BELIEVE YOUR EARS

Kirke Mechem

BELIEVE YOUR EARS

Life of a Lyric Composer

Kirke Mechem

ROWMAN & LITTLEFIELD
Lanham • Boulder • New York • London

Published by Rowman & Littlefield
A wholly owned subsidiary of The Rowman & Littlefield Publishing Group, Inc.
4501 Forbes Boulevard, Suite 200, Lanham, Maryland 20706
www.rowman.com

Unit A, Whitacre Mews, 26-34 Stannary Street, London SE11 4AB

British Library Cataloguing in Publication Information Available

Library of Congress Cataloging-in-Publication Data

Mechem, Kirke, author.
Believe your ears : life of a lyric composer / Kirke Mechem.
pages cm.
Includes index.
ISBN 978-1-4422-5076-5 (cloth : alk. paper) — ISBN 978-1-5381-0438-5 (pbk. : alk. paper) — ISBN 978-1-4422-5077-2 (ebook)
1. Mechem, Kirke. 2. Composers—United States—Biography. I. Title.
ML410.M4547A3 2015
780.92—dc23
[B]
2015008231

♾ ™ The paper used in this publication meets the minimum requirements of American National Standard for Information Sciences Permanence of Paper for Printed Library Materials, ANSI/NISO Z39.48-1992.

Printed in the United States of America

For
Donata, Katharine, Elizabeth, Edward, and Jennifer
and in loving memory of
my father, who gave me words,
and my mother, who gave me music

CONTENTS

PRELUDE

You are in your seat at a symphony concert. You loved the Bernstein overture; you look forward to the Brahms after intermission. But right now you're trapped, listening to incomprehensible cacophony and asking yourself, "Why do they keep doing this to us?"

This book will try to answer that question.

Although this is essentially a memoir of my musical life—not a history of music since 1950—the two cannot be separated. The story of *every* composer of this period must be told in the context of a chaotic musical era. After World War II, new classical music began to be dominated by atonality. Someone had apparently decided that music was simply "organized sound." Beat on a trash can, play the piano with your elbow, throw dice to decide which notes to play, or if you were so hidebound as to write old-fashioned notes, just make sure you didn't accidentally produce any melodies or anything so vulgar as rhythm. Even the kind of harmony that had been the basis of music for centuries was forbidden in progressive circles.

I will examine this phenomenon through my own experience as a composer. When this book was taking shape I had to make a decision about its format. Should it concentrate on the battle between tonality and atonality, using my personal experiences sparingly? Some suggested that would be a more influential book. I decided, however, that a narrative about my musical life would allow my opinions to emerge naturally. I have no desire to write a polemic—to pretend that my opinions are facts or proclamations. I also wanted to discuss many other aspects of the classical-music world, both in the United States and in other countries where I have lived and worked.

Moreover, my path to composition was unorthodox; it makes a good story. It has enough ups and downs to create emotion and suspense. And I believe with Goethe that "all theory is gray." An idea comes alive only when it affects the lives of real people. And as in a novel, the protagonist must have a background; all artists carry their life stories into their art. That is why this book is both a memoir and a serious discussion of how classical music shot itself in the foot. The opening chapters describe my musical background but also the literary and dramatic influences that were to play an important part in my career as a librettist and composer of operas, and as a choral composer who frequently adapted, juxtaposed, and invented diverse texts to form larger works: cycles, suites, and cantatas.

As an adolescent I played the piano mainly by ear and wrote pop songs that I hardly knew how to notate. My youth was spent as a newspaper reporter, a touring tennis player, a soldier, and a Stanford creative-writing major. I was twenty-two before I took my first music course. I began to compose, not as a musical prodigy, but as a music lover, and have always tried to maintain the point of view of a listener. I never wrote atonal music because I didn't like it. When I was young and impressionable, there was no teacher to tell me I *should* like it. I do not compose according to any theory, and while I have enjoyed teaching such skills as harmony, counterpoint, and orchestration, I have always declined to teach composition per se because it is so personal and intuitive.

My opinions did not endear me to those who marched under the revolutionary banner of progress. The history of twentieth-century music is the rise and fall of that banner. That was the century of science and technology. "Progressive" composers, quick to claim that music was a science, began their experiments in earnest, and some continue indefatigably to this day.

Those who believe that this is a dead issue—that atonality has already given way to the return of tonal music—are only partly correct. While it is true that few composers today write in Schoenberg's strict twelve-tone system, most academic music departments are still heavily invested in atonal or otherwise extremely dissonant music. Many of today's professors were taught by zealous atonalists, as were others who remain influential in the larger music community as composers, critics, and conductors.

* * *

I have come to believe that equating music with science was the root cause of the calamity that befell classical music. Those composers who considered music a science were obliged to keep up with the latest developments, experiments, and theories, however extreme or arcane. But for composers who considered music a language, communication with their listeners was of primary importance. Their compositions followed an evolutionary path and were meant to be comprehensible to music lovers of their own time. Language changes very slowly; we still attend Shakespeare's plays four hundred years after they were written. Bach's music still delights and nourishes us.

A noted paleontologist advised us not to misunderstand science. The late Stephen Jay Gould, in his 2011 book, *Full House*, attributed the inaccessibility of new music to "the misplaced value we ascribe to innovation." Progress, Gould insisted, does not significantly mark the history of life. "Natural evolution includes no principle of predictable progress or movement to greater complexity," he wrote, and went on to warn that "this perpetual striving toward novelty" may prevent any of today's composers from becoming "the Mozart of the new millennium."

I was one of the many composers still writing tonal music in the latter half of the twentieth century. Tonality had been expanded—almost redefined—by Debussy, Bartók, Stravinsky, Hindemith, and others. In no way did we feel that we were flogging a dead horse, as was sometimes charged by the more vocal avant-garde. You could see the freedom we had in the diversity of our styles. And beginning with the minimalists in the 1970s, there was a dedicated reaction against atonality. This led some young composers back to melody and harmony—even to beauty and humor. In this warmer musical climate, I chose for my fourth opera a subject known to *radiate* beauty and humor: *Pride and Prejudice*.

The twentieth century gave us much brilliant music. I do not subscribe to the narrow views of a famous 1955 book, *The Agony of Modern Music*, by Henry Pleasants. Art renews itself constantly, and music is no exception. But the late twentieth century was the first time in history that most classical-music lovers preferred music of past centuries to that of their own. I hope that this book will encourage music lovers who are bewildered or intimidated by unintelligible sounds to believe their own ears. I am not advising you to close your ears to new sounds, but simply suggesting that "experts" cannot tell you what you should or should not like. Art is not a duty. Whatever you like—tonal, atonal, jazz, or electronic—go for it! Even brash novelties can be entertaining if they don't overstay their welcome. Every new work does not have to be a masterpiece that will live for generations—but it should at least not repel you.

* * *

As a child I often went to sleep listening to my mother practice the piano. She played at least one recital or concerto every year, and we children understood that these were important events. While she was a devout Presbyterian and my father an atheist, they respected each other's beliefs. The common spiritual force in our family was music. In my adolescence, my moments of confusion or grief were assuaged by listening to a record of Ravel, Rachmaninoff, or Bach. Though I do not share my mother's religious convictions, the great poetry of the Bible and the profound music it has inspired touch me deeply; they connect me with my mother. But they also connect me with my father, who loved my mother through music just as all of their children did. I have set many of his poems to music.

Is it any wonder then that I should regard music as something sacred? I do not mean sacred in a religious sense. I mean it in the sense that truth is sacred; life is sacred. They are not to be mocked. While I love to laugh at hypocrisy, and love humor almost anywhere I find it, I am overly sensitive when I hear what I perceive to be the brutalization or deliberate obfuscation of music. This glorious art has room for endless variety, from lighthearted to tragic. Each person has a right to his or her own taste, and I recognize that just as we all come from different backgrounds, we all have different ways of listening.

And so I readily admit that my own background has conditioned what I look for in a new piece of music, whether it is my own, or someone else's. I don't want to find new music "interesting" in a purely cerebral way. I am impatient with novelty and experimentation for their own sake; I am too old to be taken in by trends or jargon: been there, heard that. Ideally I want to *love* a new piece of music. I want it to delight me, to move me to tears or laughter, to in some way take me out of myself. At the very least I must want to hear the piece again, the sooner the better. I expect as much from new music as I do from that of past centuries.

If we composers are not understood by our contemporaries, we are simply spinning our wheels, and music becomes just another plaything, a "happening," or an elitist way of putting down the uninitiated. I prefer it to be the magnificent source of beauty, joy, consolation, ingenuity, inspiration, and, yes, entertainment, that it has been for generations and was in my own family.

❈ ❈ ❈

This book does not attempt to describe or analyze my music. I don't like the kind of program note that declares that Principal Theme A is followed by Transitional Group B in the relative minor. And I cannot describe how I compose. I don't know exactly where ideas come from; sometimes they come from improvising or, more often, just from thinking musically. Often when I wake up in the morning, there's music in my head, though the music is often a solution to a compositional problem I left in my studio the day before. I vary the way I work—sometimes using the piano, sometimes not. I use an old-fashioned device called a pencil.

Writing about a piece of music is futile; you cannot describe it any more than you can describe the taste of a peach or the smell of a rose. One minute of listening is worth ten pages of description. If you click on my website—http://kirkemechem.com—you will find audio clips of nearly all the music mentioned in this book, as well as a complete catalog that lists date of composition, duration, and publisher for each piece.

I acknowledge, however, that music lovers—myself included—enjoy reading about the circumstances that give rise to composition, and about the composer's life. Why did the composer choose a certain text for a song or a particular subject for an opera? How are they adapted to music? Are there special considerations associated with writing in one genre compared to another? What are the practical difficulties of a composer's life—getting performances, publications, and commissions? I have no problem with this kind of discussion; you will find examples throughout the book.

My chief aim has been to give an accurate picture of a chaotic musical era as experienced by one composer.

I

EXPOSITION

You would think that the musically gifted child of a concert pianist would surely become proficient on the piano. In my case, unfortunately, you would be mistaken. My mother started each of us four children at the piano at age six or seven. The eldest, Rose Mary, kept at it the longest, but like many people, her love for music greatly exceeded her talent. She became a senior editor for *Sports Illustrated* magazine. My older brother, James, and younger, Richard, gave it up quickly, though they also became lifelong music lovers. James became a writer, Richard a clinical psychologist. My parents saw that I had musical talent and tried their best to get me to practice.

There were three obstacles to my piano career. First, I was obsessed with sports. Second, none of my friends played an instrument. Third, and most important, my mother had no idea how to teach me. She had never studied harmony and did not think of music in terms of how it was composed. If my father had been the musician, it would have been different. It was he who gave us lessons in writing. He was both creative and analytical; he would probably have started by asking me to invent a melody, and then helped me to figure out a couple of chords for it. But my mother relied on the old John Thompson method that taught beginners which finger to put down for each note. She was also not equipped psychologically to deal with such a strong-willed, rambunctious kid like me.

My parents finally hit upon a strategy—bribery—to use my love of sports to encourage my musical development. They promised a baseball glove if I practiced for six months. Next I was offered a football helmet for another six months' practice, then a tennis racquet, and finally a basketball. Once I had all the sports equipment, I quit practicing. One of the highlights of my boyhood sports career was playing tennis with Bill Tilden. Okay, I didn't exactly "play" with him. When I was about fourteen, Tilden was giving tennis clinics in many cities, asking the local people to supply a good junior player for the event. I was the guinea pig in Topeka, and did actually get to hit balls back and forth with the legendary master.

Topeka, the capital of Kansas, was a leafy city of about sixty-four thousand when my family moved there from Wichita, where I was born. Our home was a four-bedroom, clapboard house in a middle-class neighborhood ten blocks west of downtown. The street was made of red bricks set on edge; the large elm trees on either side converged to give the effect of a long, green canopy—it looked like a set for an Andy Hardy movie. It was within walking distance to schools, grocery stores, and my father's office. Although he was never able to finish high school, my father educated himself and became executive director of the Kansas State Historical Society. Before he ever started work, the Depression-strapped legislature cut his annual salary from $2,800 to $2,400.

My parents read books in the evening. They listened to the Metropolitan Opera broadcast on Saturdays and to the New York Philharmonic on Sundays. My mother's father had moved to Wichita after fighting for the Union in the Civil War. My mother studied piano in Munich for a year and was accepted as a Leschetizky pupil in Vienna. But when World War I broke out in 1914, she had to return home.

It's not surprising that my father fell in love with Katharine Lewis. Four years his junior, she was a beautiful girl with dark-auburn hair and a sweet disposition. She played a wide range of music. Chopin was her favorite, and she played much Beethoven and Bach. At that time, however, I preferred her pieces by Rachmaninoff, Debussy, Ravel, Bartók, de Falla, Stravinsky, Gershwin, and Copland—accessible works that whetted my appetite for twentieth-century music.

My father, Kirke Field Mechem—I am Kirke Lewis Mechem, so technically not a "junior"—had always loved music; his mother and both his sisters had studied piano. As a young man in Topeka, he was the baritone in a barbershop quartet. In 1911 the quartet sang at an event for which President William Howard Taft was the speaker. When asked where I got my musical talent, I sometimes answer, "Why, my father sang for the president!" In fact, I don't believe my father ever learned to read music, but he had the ear of a connoisseur. When discussing a piece of music he had just heard, he always described it from the point of view of the composer: "Did you notice how Beethoven kept changing that first melody?"

Dad's hair was dark, his eyes hazel, and he often looked as if he were about to tell a joke. His own father had been the tallest and youngest member of the Kansas Senate before he was killed in a railroad accident when my father was eight. Dad had a delightful sense of humor and a deep hatred of injustice, which may have been the result of being forced into poverty after having grown up in a cultured, affluent family. It was the Charles Dickens syndrome: a boy suddenly thrown into a lower social class develops a compulsion to make something of himself. My father became a reporter, a magazine publisher, a fine poet, a novelist, and a playwright. When the Great Depression killed my father's magazine, William Allen White helped get him the job as head of the state historical society.

It wasn't until I was about fifteen, when popular music began to play a part in my social life, that I came back to the piano—but in quite a different way. I will return to that shortly. First I need to mention one other circumstance that kept me from concentrating on piano or anything else: too many talents. I was in danger of becoming the proverbial jack-of-all-trades, master of none. In addition to being good at sports, I loved drawing, acting, and, as far back as the age of nine, newspaper work.

My father had taught me to type at an early age. In the summer that I turned nine, I began to produce a newspaper, *The Lane Local* (we lived on Lane Street), which I continued for three summers. With my "assistants"—siblings and friends—I visited every house in the neighborhood to gather news: weddings, vacations, visitors, cat funerals—nothing was too insignificant.

After a brief period as a fledgling cartoonist, producing sports stories as comic books, I decided to be a sports broadcaster. I discovered that I could attach the end of an old garden hose to our Victrola phonograph, string the hose through a slightly open window, attach a kitchen funnel to the other end of the hose in our yard, and by talking into the funnel my voice would come from the radio. Dreams of glory! I really did "broadcast" complete fantasy games, thrilled that I was "talking on the radio."

I sold the afternoon daily newspaper on a street corner downtown until a bigger, tougher kid said it was "his" corner and chased me off. All three of us boys had paper routes after school, and I sold magazines door-to-door. In high school I worked at the post office during the Christmas holidays. But none of this seemed arduous. We didn't consider ourselves poor because everybody was poor. At least my father had a job. Unlike today, that meant he could support a family.

My happy boyhood came to an end when I entered junior high school. I had been skipped a half-grade in elementary school, which made me significantly younger than my junior-high, midyear classmates, many of whom had flunked or transferred. This, combined with puberty, sent me into a tailspin that I prefer to forget. (But I do remember winning a fight against "Hook" Snook by breaking his finger with my jaw.)

Mercifully, my parents took me out of school when I graduated from junior high in January, so that I began high school the next fall with kids my own age. The misery of those three years as a misfit ended abruptly, and I was once again a thriving, enterprising boy, but trying too hard to make up for lost time. I wanted to be in everything—sports, drama, journalism, student government—not to mention trying desperately to be liked by girls.

My musical development resumed in high school. Everyone followed the latest popular songs on the radio show *Your Hit Parade* and danced to them at school parties and proms. I had always been able to play popular tunes by ear with rudimentary chords, but I had no system. My girlfriend's brother, Judson Goodrich, could play pop songs fluently, so I asked him to teach me more about chords.

"It's simple," he said, and demonstrated on the piano in the key of C. "There are only four kinds of chords (triads): major, like this (C-E-G); then if you lower the middle note a half step, it's called a minor chord. And if you also lower the top note a half step, that's a diminished chord. Go back to the major chord, then raise the top note a half step, and you've got an augmented chord. That's all there is! Oh, and you should also know that for the 'dominant' chord—the one that starts on the fifth note of the scale (G-B-D)—you can add another note two steps higher

(F), which is called a 'seventh' chord, and you can keep on adding notes like that until you have a 'ninth' chord, an 'eleventh,' or a 'thirteenth.'"

That was the only harmony "lesson" I had until many years later when I took a course at Stanford and saw a harmony book for the first time. But crude as this lesson was, it gave names and a system to what I had already been conscious of. I was a kid with a new toy.

From that moment on, I spent hours at the piano. My family complained, "You can't get through to him." I learned to transpose songs from one key to another. I worked out the harmonies of popular songs I heard. It dawned on me that nearly all of them were thirty-two measures long. "Well, gee whiz," I said in my best Mickey Rooney/Andy Hardy imitation, "I can write songs myself!" (Could "Let's put on a show!" have been far behind?) My first attempt was a song with dreadfully trite words and music called "Sunny Sunday." Just as my youthful ego had prompted me to list myself as publisher, editor, chief-reporter, business manager, printer, and artist on the masthead of *The Lane Local*, I had the hubris to write my own lyrics.

There was a problem, though: I didn't know how to write the music down. I didn't think my mother could help, so I decided to teach myself. In those days, the sheet music of any song that might become a best seller was immediately available at music stores, even in Topeka. I bought several popular songs and studied them (and my mother's piano music) until I understood enough about vocal and piano notation to write down my own miserable tunes.

Topeka High School had a large orchestra with full string sections, an even larger marching band, many instrumental ensembles, and five choral groups. I must say with great chagrin that when I was a student I never set foot in the music wing. I played on the basketball team, but gave that up to concentrate on tennis. I was in school plays, was elected to the school council, wrote skits and plays for school assemblies, and became editor of the school newspaper. That's not the way to become a composer. I lost the very years of practice one needs to become a virtuoso performer, and I later required several years of study to learn to read orchestral scores, a skill I could have acquired in a fraction of the time had I begun earlier.

But there is another way to look at this: only someone with an enormous love for music would give up so many other talents to follow the profession he had least prepared himself for. Many musicians say, "I didn't choose music; it chose me." That's not true in my case; I *chose* music, and when I did, I was old enough to know clearly what I was doing.

* * *

By June 1942, almost every able-bodied man between the ages of eighteen and twenty-nine was already serving in the military. That included newspapermen, which explains how, between my junior and senior years, I was hired by the *Topeka Daily Capital* as a full-time, assistant sports editor. Most of what I did was desk work—editing the Associated Press stories, writing headlines, and making up the sports pages for print—but I also covered minor local events.

When I learned that the aging Joe Louis was going to act as referee for a wrestling match, I decided to interview him. The "Brown Bomber" was considered the greatest heavyweight boxer in history. I had listened to his championship fights on the radio; I idolized him. Any experienced reporter would have phoned ahead to make an appointment, but that never occurred to this seventeen-year-old greenhorn. Between bouts I found the great man talking with admirers in the hall, so I seized the moment to crowd in among them. With pencil and pad in hand, I finally got Louis's attention. Incredibly, I hadn't even considered what I would ask him. I was so overwhelmed by his magnificence and my insignificance that all I could blurt out was, "How do you like Topeka, Joe?"

It was around that time that I decided I wasn't cut out to be a newspaperman.

2

MILITARY MUSIC

My military service was undistinguished. It belongs in this book only because for two and a half years I had a great deal of free time to continue my musical self-instruction.

I reported for duty at Fort Leavenworth in November 1943 and within a week almost died of spinal meningitis. Meningitis may have been the luckiest thing that ever happened to me. It deferred for four months the beginning of my basic training and shipment to overseas duty, which meant that by the time I arrived in France I was well behind the fighting.

I had been treated with sulfa drugs in the Fort Leavenworth hospital for a month and was given a month's furlough to recuperate. Returning for duty I still weighed only 125 pounds—as I am over six feet tall I looked like a scarecrow—so I was given a job as a clerk at the base. After two months I was back to my normal weight, and I asked to be transferred into regular basic training. Patriotism or bravery had little to do with it. I was simply afraid that after the war I would have to admit I had done my service ninety miles from home.

I was sent to Camp Hood, Texas, for training in a tank-destroyer unit. The only interesting break from that was doing voice impersonations of famous people in variety shows at the Officers' Club. Most of the officers were too drunk to notice that I was a rank amateur. But years later, this gift of mimicry served me well in composing comic-opera caricatures.

* * *

My first few months overseas were spent in England, mostly in the southern resort city of Bournemouth. Palm trees in England! I soon found the Conservatory of Music, where there were many pianos with almost no one to play them. The director was kind enough to let me use one of the practice rooms whenever the building was open.

Twice I was permitted to go to London on a three-day pass. The city was devastated from the Nazi bombing; ruined buildings, piles of stone, and empty lots were everywhere. The V-1 "Buzz Bombs" (guided missiles) were still occasionally falling on the city when I visited early in March. By that time, however, most of the launching sites had been overrun by Allied forces, and the British civilians made light of the bombs, calling them "Doodlebugs." But they had caused over twenty thousand casualties, and I wasn't so sanguine as the locals were.

A pleasant memory was a free lunchtime recital by the famous pianist Dame Myra Hess. I had often heard my mother play Dame Myra's transcription of Bach's "Jesu, Joy of Man's Desiring," and felt a personal affinity. The weather was cold and rainy. Frequent coughing began a minute or two after she had begun a Beethoven sonata. She stopped playing, and with a friendly smile said, "It's terrible weather, isn't it? Why don't we all have a good cough, and then I'll just start from the beginning again." I have never heard another musician deal with interruption so graciously.

Later, I made a sentimental trip to Wimbledon, a magnet for all tennis enthusiasts. I was in luck. Mary Hardwick, the British champion, was having tea with a friend in the café; I recognized her from having seen her play on tour in Topeka. When I introduced myself, she invited me to join them and asked about my tennis and army experiences. The English had lost so many young men in both wars that they had an especially tender feeling for boys in uniform far away from home.

In France I always looked for a piano or an army field organ—a kind of portable harmonium with bellows operated by the feet—where I could either try out the harmonies of songs I had heard or write my own songs. A clerk in our company overseas was a professional musician. Casper Boragine, a violinist and composer of light orchestral pieces, had been conductor of the Newark Sinfonietta. I was lucky to get his help on my songs, but it was sometimes frustrating.

"Kirke, you have good ideas, but you don't know what to do with them," he told me. I was outraged when he took one of my "good ideas" and made his own song out of it. He said he had done it as an example for me to learn from, but all I learned was to keep my musical ideas to myself. Casper was a short, rotund thirty-eight-year-old; drafting him showed how desperate the army was for manpower. He had a good sense of humor and the thickest New Jersey accent I had ever heard. Once I said to him, "Casper, you keep using a word I don't understand—'dubodius'—what does that mean?"

"Whaddaya talkin' about? Ever'body knows 'at. Look, s'pose I'm walkin' down da street wid a couple of my buddies. I decide to go home, but I says to 'em, 'Youse guys go on to da movies—dubodius.' Da *both* of youse guys—get it, stupid?"

❆ ❆ ❆

When the war in Europe ended, I was shipped back to the U.S. West Coast to prepare for duty in the Japanese war. But the Japanese surrendered before I embarked. (The Germans had also surrendered just as I was about to enter Germany. I could weave quite a heroic story around those events—if only two million other soldiers didn't have the same story.) I ended up in Special Services at Fort Ord, California, writing songs for USO shows. I was by that time a master-sergeant, so I came and went as I pleased, spending most of my time in beautiful Carmel-by-the-Sea.

I teamed with another soldier to write a musical. It was pretty bad and, fortunately, never produced. My friend wrote the "book." After he took the score to New York and showed it to friends in the business, he reported back that his friends thought my songs were corny. They were right. The show included such immortal titles as "The Colonel's Daughter" and "Waiting for the Telephone to Ring." The best song I wrote in the days of my musical illiteracy was for my lovely girlfriend, Martha Goodrich (now Mrs. Arthur Coate). Here are the words of the nineteen-year-old soldier's love song:

> *Verse:* When winter winds blow warmer
> From a touch of the golden sun,
> You feel that the world is awaiting
> Something . . . someone:
> It waits with great impatience,
> As if it were something new
> For springtime to want to be dancing
> With love . . . with you.

Refrain: What good is spring without you?
If birds cannot sing about you?
How green without sun is a country lane?
How red a rose without the rain?
Why must this day remind me
Of days I have left behind me?
What joy to my heart does an April bring?
Without your love, what good is spring?

"What Good Is Spring?" was inspired by Shakespeare's Sonnet 98, "From you have I been absent in the spring." Years later I set the real sonnet as a madrigal in my cycle, *Five Centuries of Spring*. When I tell you that the words to this early song are better than the music, you will understand how much music I needed to learn. Of course, I didn't know that yet.

A performance of the song was reviewed in the *Carmel Pine Cone;* it was my first newspaper review. The critic praised the counterpoint of my Rachmaninoff-style piano arrangement. I took my songs to Capitol Music Publishers in Hollywood without a clue that it was a fool's errand. A couple of avuncular men in the office looked over my manuscripts and remarked, "Sergeant, you're paying way too much to have this music duplicated." I had made photocopies, the only method I knew of. In those pre-Xerox days, photocopies cost about a dollar per page—an enormous sum then. I had sent all my songs to the Library of Congress to be copyrighted—dreams of glory again.

God help me if they ever surface!

3

KEY CHANGE

The Accidental Composer

I did not choose Stanford solely because of its academic reputation. In 1938 my father had been invited to attend the premiere of his play, *John Brown,* at Stanford; it had won the Maxwell Anderson Award for Verse Drama, a national competition that was administered by Stanford. My parents were impressed by the university, but my principal motivation was to play tennis on what had been the most successful college team in the country.

I played four years for Stanford, becoming the number-one player in my junior year. This gave me the honor of being beaten almost every week of the season by a nationally ranked player. One week I lost 6–3, 6–3 to Art Larsen (University of San Francisco), who won the national championship at Forest Hills the following summer; the next week I was beaten 6–4, 6–4 by Herb Flam (UCLA), whom Larsen defeated in the championship finals. (I list the scores because I'm proud to have won any games at all.) With my old friend from Kansas, Lucien Barbour, as my doubles partner, we did manage to beat one highly ranked team, Hugh Stewart and Gil Shea, playing then at the University of Southern California. (They were so angry that they murdered us in our next school match.) During the summers, I won a number of state championships and the Midwest Open against far less hazardous opponents. But I gave up tournament tennis in 1950 at the age of twenty-four. By this time I was hooked on music. Choosing between it and tennis was a no-brainer.

From the description above, you would have no idea how much I loved tennis when I was growing up. Every day of rain was a lost day. I loved the competition. I had always been a competitive kid and was impatient to get onto the court to begin the battle. Six or seven years after not playing at all, I took up the game again just for fun. It's a wonderful game.

I entered Stanford as an English major, intending to follow in my father's footsteps as a writer. I was good at writing essays and term papers, but later, in the creative-writing classes, I began to wonder why I had majored in English at all. My first roommate at Stanford was Clay Putman, who was already writing brilliant short stories. He had read every novel I had ever heard of and many I had not. How did I think I was going to be a creative writer when I had never read Hemingway, Fitzgerald, Faulkner, or most other contemporary masters? During my army years, by chance I had read three important coming-of-age novels. I think I picked Samuel Butler's *The Way of All Flesh* out of an army library because I thought it might be racy—ditto for D. H. Lawrence's *Sons and Lovers.* I had heard of Somerset Maugham but don't know why I read *Of Human Bondage*—same reason, probably. All three books seemed like masterpieces to me, and they freed me from a kind of restrictive thinking I had grown up with in the Bible Belt. But I read them as a reader, not as a writer.

I don't have the temperament of a novelist, who must be a keen observer. In most situations I'm not an observer, but an actor, a participant. Drama is the only genre in which I could possibly have succeeded as a writer. I had a good ear for dialogue, could write light verse that sometimes passed for clever, and was always a good mimic. Those are scant recommendations for a serious playwright, though they did come in handy when I began to write opera librettos.

I took a stimulating course, The American Novel, from Wallace Stegner. He was a tennis fan who often came to see our matches, and a music lover. His presence in the department, however, did not make up for the deadly academic courses English majors had to take. A typical daily assignment was to read fifty pages of Wordsworth's poetry. The next day, the stuffy professor would give a test simply to find out if we had read all fifty pages; the questions were on the order of "What color was Lucy's locket?"

❊ ❊ ❊

Before 1947, Stanford had no music department; music had been a division of Humanities. The excellent, young faculty members of the new department came from Juilliard, Harvard, Curtis, Columbia, and the Budapest Conservatory. Because the department was new, classes were small. My theory courses were like private lessons, often with only four students in a class.

For non-musicians I should explain that "theory" courses in music are not theoretical, but practical. Harmony and counterpoint, the main elements in music theory, deal with the nuts and bolts of music: how scales and chords are used and how melodies and musical forms are constructed. Taught by a good teacher, a theory course is a hands-on study of how music has actually been written by composers of different periods.

Harold Schmidt, the choral man, taught the first theory course I ever had. It was at the beginning of my sophomore year, when I was still an English major. I was curious to know what a course in "harmony" was. Schmidt did not use a textbook so much as he did the Bach chorales, which we sang in class. I learned very few new chords in my years of theory classes, as my ear, my self-tuition in jazz, and my mother's piano scores had already brought me into contact with advanced tonal harmony. But classical terminology was different, and for the first time I began to think of chords as products of multiple melodies.

This became clear when Schmidt insisted that everyone in his classes sing in the chorus. It is no exaggeration to say that the first rehearsal changed my life. I remember in particular two choruses we sang from Handel's *L'Allegro:* "Or Let the Merry Bells Ring Round" and "These Delights If Thou Canst Give." As I sang my part, I was surrounded by other moving lines coming from every direction: the third of the chord from over there, the fifth from the sopranos, and they were all *melodies!* You must remember that I had never played in an orchestra or sung in a chorus before. My music-making had been limited to the piano keyboard: vertical chords, black and white. Here suddenly were multilayered, moving melodies that produced chords—Technicolor and 3-D! From that moment I became infatuated with choral music and began to

understand the beauty of contrapuntal writing, whether vocal or instrumental.

It is sad to think that such a fundamental experience—making music
as part of an ensemble—should have come to me so late. The only
possible good that can be said of that delay is that I can easily identify
with the amateur choral singer's exaltation at performing great music.
This, too, helps explain my strong attachment to melodies that can be
sung.

That first harmony class was so much fun—and so easy—I decided
to continue taking theory courses. Harmony and counterpoint are required everywhere for music majors, many of whom—especially singers
and instrumentalists who don't play the piano—find these courses the
most difficult. For me they were like play. Writing my assignments
became the happiest moments of my school life, and I found myself
understanding more and more about the wonderful music I heard. I
began to pay more attention to all music. I wanted to be able to create it
myself. If music gave such pleasure and deep happiness to people,
surely that was a good path to follow.

Leonard Ratner took over the theory classes and proved to be an
extraordinary teacher. He taught living music, not rules from a book.
When we studied Mozart's works, we analyzed his sonatas to discover
why they sounded like Mozart and not Bach or Chopin. Then, as all
young composers have done, we tried to imitate various styles of the
past. Ratner corrected not only our technical mistakes, but also our
stylistic anachronisms. He continued this method of teaching through
the Impressionists and the twelve-tone music of Schoenberg. Thirty
years later, this helped me to parody various operatic styles in my comic
opera *Tartuffe*.

Ratner's enthusiasm for writing music was infectious. In counterpoint class, we loved to watch him compose a three-part invention in
the style of Bach on the blackboard. He told us what he was doing as he
went along, why he made this choice and not another. We were all so
caught up in it that none of us (including Ratner) could leave the room
when the bell rang. I saw the importance of developing my inner ear so
that I could compose away from the piano when I wished to.

His enthusiasm also extended to the analysis of musical form. Instead of the kind of dry analysis one finds in books and program notes,
his was a delighted discovery of the ways in which genius worked to

create marvels and surprises. His sense of humor—similar to my
father's—appealed greatly to me; it was another thing that made music
theory my favorite subject.

Ratner's influence was also important in what he did *not* do. He did
not try to convince us that traditional tonality was dead. Many music
schools at that time were so sure that atonality was the music of the
future that they stopped teaching classic harmony. While Ratner did
have us study a few atonal and serial works, he did not express his
opinion of their value.

I was still an English major throughout my sophomore and junior
years, but continued attending theory classes and singing in the chorus.
As the San Francisco Symphony did not yet have its own chorus, the
major choral-orchestral works were sung either by the Stanford chorus
or that of UC–Berkeley. My love for choral music was greatly magnified
by singing Beethoven's Ninth, Brahms's *Schicksalslied*, Handel's *Messiah,* and other works with the San Francisco Symphony. Our chorus
also performed a concert at Stanford each quarter. Schmidt's choral
groups sang a great variety of music of all periods—Kodaly's *Te Deum*
impressed me greatly, as had Bruckner's. Just as Ratner was the perfect
teacher for the budding instrumental composer, Schmidt was ideal for
the future choral composer—he exposed me to an immense number of
works, old and new, European and American. He was more interested
in giving his students and audiences a wide range of music than in
perfecting a few works. We never memorized; Schmidt relied more on
inspiration than on detailed rehearsing, though of course he had to do
that, too. He was an experienced tenor and violinist, and managed
through example and enthusiasm to bring our choruses up to a high
level of performance.

At the end of my junior year I changed my major to music. During
my fourth and fifth years at Stanford I made up the music-history
classes I had missed, went on to Ratner's composition class, and took
one quarter of conducting and two of orchestration from Sandor Salgo—all that was offered. For the composition class I wrote three madrigals on poems by Sara Teasdale: "Let It Be Forgotten"; "I Shall Not
Care"; and "Song (Love Me with Your Whole Heart)." These did not
receive any mention in the department's composition contest, but a few
years later they were published—together with two of my other Teas-

dale madrigals—as *The Winds of May*, op. 17. After sixty years they are still in print and often performed.

❁ ❁ ❁

I also began writing songs for the student Gaieties, Stanford's elaborate variety show that is given every fall. Bill Barnes, a few years older than I, orchestrated the dozen songs and conducted the twenty-eight-piece professional orchestra. We became friends; he chose a number of my songs for the 1949 show, and recommended that I be hired to orchestrate and direct the show the following year.

I had never orchestrated anything outside of class, where our efforts were not performed or even rehearsed, and I had never conducted a single note. How I had the nerve to take on this assignment while attending classes, I'll never know. Fools rush in. Bill got me started by showing me his scores from the previous show. The orchestra included small string sections, flute, four clarinets doubling saxophones, horn, three trumpets, a trombone, percussion, and piano. I moved into a little shack next to the tennis courts—thanks to my good friend, Don Auxier—and somehow got the job done in less than two months. It included a ten-minute "Carnival Ballet" score (think Richard Rodgers meets Richard Strauss). Before the first orchestra rehearsal, I had a horrible dream: the musicians took one look at their parts, put down their instruments, and laughed uproariously.

But it all went off without a hitch, and even my orchestrations received critical praise. My conducting was dreadfully stiff, as one would expect from a beginner, but as the music was not difficult, the professional players had no trouble staying together. Looking back, I realize that if Bill Barnes had not befriended me and believed in my ability more than I did, I would have left Stanford without ever having heard a note of mine played by an orchestra, or having conducted in any real-life situation.

With the money the orchestration job paid me I was finally able to buy an old car—my first, a 1941 Plymouth. It didn't last long, however, and made no difference in my social life, as I still had little money. (My tuition and books were paid for by the GI Bill of Rights.) The girls I dated knew we weren't going to dinner in San Francisco.

One of my best friends at Stanford was a lovely and talented pianist, Cynthia Troxell, whose father was a professor of economics and had attended Washburn College in Topeka. Her mother introduced me to the poetry of Sara Teasdale. My visits to their home always restored my spirits. Cynthia later married Philippe Dunoyer, who became head of the North American division of the French *Total* Oil Company. She also became a painter of marvelous watercolors. Philippe is a good amateur pianist, and he and Cynthia have remained our lifelong friends.

Another friend was Claire Collins (now Skall), a beautiful soprano who loved tennis. She sang a number of my songs, but complained that they were too cynical. I had vigorously tried to live down the "corny" epithet by cultivating a Cole Porter–like sophistication.

"Why don't you write something *beautiful* for a change?" she asked. That was how the soprano-mezzo duet in my opera, *The Rivals,* first saw the light of day—as a song for soprano (and it can still be sung as a soprano solo). It's now called "Lydia's Romance," but the original title was "My Love's a Song."

While on the subject of recycling early pieces into later works (which all composers do), I should mention that my most popular aria, "Fair Robin I Love," from *Tartuffe*, had its origin in a song I wrote in my first-year harmony class to the John Dryden poem "Fair Iris I Love." In its student version it had the same melody but a very simple keyboard accompaniment. The fa-la-la's for the voice, the "fickle"-sounding sixteenth notes for woodwinds, and the coda were all added for the opera aria.

The Ram's Head Theatrical Society, the student organization in charge of producing the Gaieties each fall, also sponsored a contest for a student-written musical that they would produce in the spring. They hired me as music director and orchestrator for the show to be given in the spring of 1951. I had already begun writing a musical myself, and thought that being the music director might give me a leg up in the competition. I was wrong.

My musical was called *Save the Nation*, a satire on college education. Highly imitative of Gershwin's *Of Thee I Sing*, its story revolved around an old tycoon who plans to make a fortune by enticing veterans to enter his new university. One of the enticements is a chorus of beautiful girls who sing such ditties as this:

> We have read the works of Nietzsche
> And we think that Plato's peachy.
> We're up on all the Greek cosmology;
> We never shirk or dawdle,

When it comes to Aristotle;
We love to study deep philosophy.

I really couldn't blame Ram's Head for choosing to produce a different
show. I had never been active in the organization, so why would the
committee choose me to be the author of the script and lyrics, composer of the music, orchestrator, and conductor as well? (This wasn't *The
Lane Local*.) I asked permission for Bill Barnes to take over my musical
duties, which he kindly did. When I saw the production of the winning
entry by Wally White, I had to admit that it was a better show than
mine—not musically, perhaps, but, unlike my own, White's characters
were not stereotypical. I hadn't yet heard the old theater definition of
"satire"—"that which closes in New Haven"—but I learned it then.

The direction of one's life often depends upon a small, chance detail.
How often do we say, "None of this would have happened if only . . . !"
In my case, what if my first harmony course had not been taught by
Harold Schmidt? Would I have ever sung in a chorus or written for
chorus? Would I have had a teacher who took a personal interest in my
development—one who believed in me from the start? Would I have
become a musician? Schmidt was my mentor, later my boss, and my
friend for life. He tried out my first attempts at choral composition with
one or another of his choral groups. He often invited me to his home,
especially at Thanksgiving when I could not afford to make the trip back
to Kansas. I knew his son and daughter when they were children, and
we have been friends ever since.

Harold Schmidt at that time was in his mid-forties. He had a cookie-
duster mustache on a flat-cheeked, German face. His receding hair was
light brown; his eyes were gray-blue. He was of medium height and just
over medium weight, but there was nothing medium about his personality. Usually jovial and often excitable, he could be brought to a boil if
things went wrong. One of the most significant things he did for me
occurred during my last quarter at Stanford. I had not yet made plans
for the future when the head of the department called me into his
office.

"Kirke, where do you expect to go to graduate school?"

I told him I hadn't decided.

"Well, I think we have the best spot for you right here at Stanford.
Next year we are beginning a program to train music teachers for junior

colleges. As you are not professionally accomplished on any instrument, teaching in a junior college should be a good solution for you."

I said that I would think it over. When I next saw Schmidt, I repeated this conversation. He hit the ceiling. "Don't listen to that nonsense! He only wants students for his new pet program. You're going to Harvard to study with Randall Thompson and Walter Piston."

I took the entrance exam that summer in Topeka and was soon notified that I had been accepted. But first I had to teach myself to read German because the Harvard music department required reading proficiency in French, which I had studied, and in German, which I had not.

4

COUNTERPOINT

What Is American Music?

Either I was a poor teacher or a slow learner; in any case, I failed Harvard's German exam. That turned out to be another great stroke of luck, right up there with catching meningitis, as I'll explain later. In the short term, however, it meant that one of my courses the first semester had to be German, not music.

Still, I was able to take choral composition and a class on Handel's choral music from Randall Thompson, and to begin sixteenth-century polyphony with A. Tillman Merritt, a course that met five days a week for the entire school year. This was a challenging and valuable course for learning choral counterpoint. I also learned a great deal from Thompson's courses.

Thompson, then about fifty-two, was probably the best-known choral composer in the country; his "Alleluia" was sung all over the world and still is. He had received me in his office—a pleasant music department tradition for greeting new graduate students—on my second day at Harvard. His hair, parted near the middle, was already white; he wore round, wire-rim glasses and had something of a patrician manner about him. He put me at ease by asking my advice about a new tennis court his family was building at their summer home. I was not acquainted with the Boston-Brahmin accent and thought he was British. (He wasn't a born Bostonian, but I wouldn't have known the difference.)

Thompson's choral composition class was something I had looked forward to. I had sung many of his works at Stanford, as Harold Schmidt was both a friend and fan of his. Like Tillman Merritt, Thompson insisted that his students start over at the beginning. I learned later that he was annoyed by young composers who wrote for chorus in dissonant and atonal styles without ever learning the basics of vocal writing or counterpoint.

Our first assignment was to make a setting of Psalm 100 ("Make a Joyful Noise unto the Lord"), using only triads in root position! Several weeks later he asked us to write a short choral piece that used imitation at various time and pitch intervals. I took some of the melodic material I had used in the first assignment, found various ways to employ it in imitation, and made this the final section of an entire motet on Psalm 100. This became one of my first published pieces, op. 2, no. 1; it has been recorded and often sung by the Mormon Tabernacle Choir.

Thompson also gave us helpful advice on the use of imitative counterpoint. (A round, such as "Three Blind Mice," is a simple example of that kind of melodic imitation.) He stressed the importance of first writing down potential subjects (melodies), then trying to discover—in advance of the actual composing process—all the imitative possibilities inherent in the subject. That is, can a second voice imitate the melody—before it has come to an end—an octave higher, or a fifth or fourth higher or lower, creating harmonies that make sense to the ear? Or can the second part (or a third or fourth part) enter one beat after the first begins? After one measure? He suggested we also try augmentation (the imitation twice as slow as the original), diminution (twice as fast), and mirror imitation (upside down).

It is important to remark here that all of these contrapuntal devices presuppose that one is writing in a tonal idiom—but not necessarily that of an earlier period. If there is no recognizable harmonic basis, counterpoint is one-dimensional. Many atonal composers use imitative counterpoint, but it sounds arbitrary to me. In my opinion, this is a serious limitation for atonal music—it lacks the magical interplay between harmony and counterpoint. Harmonic progression is the heartbeat of counterpoint. If no structural harmony is apparent to the ear—granting that harmony has evolved—then there is little pleasure in hearing contrapuntal lines. I'm reminded of Robert Frost's comment on free verse: "I'd just as soon play tennis without a net."

On hearing a Bach contrapuntal work, we sometimes pretend we can't tell which came first, the melodies or the harmonies, so perfect do both seem to be. We know, of course, that the harmony came first—intuitively, not necessarily planned in advance. In Bach's day, it would never have occurred to a composer to write *any* kind of music without a firm harmonic basis. But Bach's genius made fugues and other contrapuntal music unfold so naturally that we sometimes forget what virtuoso skill is required in this balancing act. If you compare Bach's contrapuntal works with his freer style (the fugues with the preludes, for instance) you will see that they have a similar harmonic basis. You can make a clear tonal analysis of the fugues; it just requires more allowance to be made for Bach's imaginative use of non-chord tones, such as passing tones, suspensions, and appoggiaturas. This is all the evidence we need to know that Bach's counterpoint was harmonically conceived—as was the counterpoint of every composer until the twentieth century.

❀ ❀ ❀

Note to the reader: This book is intended for anyone interested in music—professionals or those who just enjoy listening. I have tried to find a balance that will neither insult the knowledgeable nor bewilder the less informed, but each reader may occasionally find more—or less—technical detail than desired. If you did not understand everything in the foregoing paragraph, please don't lose heart. Such detail will be kept to a minimum.

❀ ❀ ❀

Walter Piston, a student of Nadia Boulanger in Paris, was one of the leading American instrumental composers of the postwar era. In the spring semester I took his composition class. We were encouraged to compose anything for which we could provide a performance in class. I enlisted a couple of my violinist friends to play duets that I wrote each week or two. They were later published as *Suite for Two Violins*, op. 4. After having played three of these duets, the violinists appeared yet again with a new one, and Piston remarked, "Mr. Mechem is grinding them out." This sentence became a maxim among my colleagues and is still repeated by my wife on appropriate occasions.

One of the duets—No. 4—apparently struck Piston's fancy, for he asked that it be played again, after which he pronounced it "very musical"—high praise from him. He pointed out (without seeing the score) that while my passacaglia melody was in a rather free G minor, the counter subject was in A minor, and then G-sharp minor. That was news to me, as I never intentionally write in two keys at once. But Piston's ear was true; the notes of the upper part could belong to A minor, then to G-sharp minor. However, I was simply writing a counterpoint to embellish the subject with interesting and emotionally apposite harmony.

Walter Piston was a genuine, pipe-smoking Maine type, a man of few words. The best example of this came in a concert-lecture in which Piston and visiting composer Aaron Copland played their own works and answered questions from a moderator. One question was, "What is American music?" Copland listed many characteristics: syncopation and "blues" notes from jazz, big-city bustle, folk music redolent of the wide, open spaces of the prairies, spirituals from the days of slavery, marches and other upbeat music typical of the optimism of America, and quiet hymns from the Shakers and other American sects. When it was Piston's turn, he drawled, "Well, I guess you could say American music is music written by Americans."

Copland did not teach any classes that semester, but he did moderate a student-composer concert in which a choral piece of mine, "Let All Mortal Flesh Keep Silence: Variations on an Ancient French Melody," was sung. I had written it as an assignment for Randall Thompson's class. The counterpoint builds up variation by variation, but the piece is resolutely diatonic and euphonious. Copland remarked that it was beautifully written for the chorus, but he hoped I would soon enter the twentieth century. The piece was later published as op. 2, no. 2. I'm sure that "Make a Joyful Noise" would have made a better impression on Copland. Nevertheless, when concertmaster Jacob Krachmalnick introduced me to him at a San Francisco Symphony rehearsal thirteen years later, Copland remembered the piece.

At Harvard I also failed to impress another famous composer—Richard Rodgers, the writer of many Broadway hits. My father had told me about a magazine article that pictured Rodgers as a generous, warm-hearted man, just the sort (my father thought) who would be happy to help a young songwriter. So after Rodgers delivered a speech in Paine Hall, I offered him a small package of my songs. He recoiled in horror. "Oh my God," he said, "my lawyer would kill me if I even *touched* that envelope!" So much for warm, fuzzy magazine articles about celebrities.

In Rodgers's defense, I must add that his refusal was justified. Many a famous songwriter has been sued for plagiarism on the slimmest of grounds.

I was not able to take Piston's fugue class for credit because it was a continuation from the first semester, when my German-language problem had interfered. I was permitted to audit the class, however, and I attended every session. Piston's final exam was to write a three-part fugue in any style we wished. Mine was a Hindemith-influenced andante. It found favor with Piston and the class members, so in 1955 I made it the middle movement of a *Trio for Oboe, Clarinet and Bassoon*, published as op. 8. I would like to add here that Piston's *Counterpoint* text is an excellent introduction to the subject. And although I never studied orchestration with him, his book on the subject has been my guide, along with the older but still valuable books by Forsythe and Rimsky-Korsakov. I regret to say, however, that I have found Piston's harmony textbook confusing and not very helpful for beginning students.

Toward the end of the spring semester, I put into practice what I had learned from Tillman Merritt's class by entering a six-part motet in the Boott Prize competition for best vocal work, which had not had a winner for several years. My piece was inspired by a Sweelinck antiphonal work I had sung at Stanford, "Or Sus, Serviteurs du Seigneur." It won the prize, and this helped me believe I was on the right track.

* * *

As I had failed the first German test, I had to extend my time at Harvard, taking summer courses in order to be eligible for the master's degree. But as I have already written, that turned out to be good luck. In the first meeting of a course given by the eminent musicologist Curt Sachs, I spotted a beautiful brunette. The next day, however, she wasn't there. Luckily, she turned up again in the summer-school chorus.

After rehearsal, I broke the ice with "Why didn't you come back to the musicology class?" which I doubt will go down in history as a great pickup line.

"I decided to take a different course."

We went to the Oxford Grill off Harvard Square, but I have no idea what we ate or drank, so beautiful and friendly was she. All I remember is that she spotted a praying mantis on my shoulder, a creature unknown to me. Now, thankfully, I know that it is a harbinger of glorious destiny.

As I walked her back to her dorm, she asked what I was studying.

"Music."

"Oh. Who are you studying with?"

"I came to study choral composition with Randall Thompson. I've sung a lot of his music."

"Really? So have I. Is he a good teacher?"

"Well, I've learned a lot from him, but I don't think his heart is in teaching. I've learned more from studying his compositions."

"That's interesting. What's wrong with his teaching?"

"Nothing, really. He just isn't particularly enthusiastic."

"That doesn't sound so bad. What else?"

"He's sometimes a little unforgiving about unimportant things."

"I see. But you did learn from him?"

"Of course. But why are you so interested in Randall Thompson's teaching method?"

"He's my uncle."

It took a while to forgive her for leading me on. Her name was Donata Coletti; her mother was the sister of Randall Thompson's wife, and her father was the well-known Boston sculptor Joseph Coletti.

I got even with her after our first real date, a British movie on campus. I came out of the theater speaking in my best upper-crust English accent, which, I must say, has fooled a few people.

"Why are you speaking with that British accent?"

"Oh, was I? I reahlly didn't notice."

"You're still doing it."

"I'm tedibly sorry. You see, I lived in England until I was eleven."

"*You did?!* But that's amazing."

"When I see a British flick I cahn't help sliding back into the old pattern."

"Is it hard to switch back and forth?"

"Not really. Once I get going one way or the other it comes naturally."

I later found her to be such an honest, trusting person that it was a crime to take advantage of her gullibility. I eventually told her the truth, and she didn't seem to mind exchanging a cultivated Brit for a Kansas bumpkin. And I forgave *her* little trick.

We didn't see as much of each other that summer as I would have liked. But in the last couple of weeks we sometimes studied together, and grew fond of one another. But I was going back to Kansas, and she had two more years before graduating from Smith. We wrote fairly often for a year, but long-distance relationships are hard to sustain. Nevertheless, I ask the reader not to give up on this romance.

* * *

The most valuable course I had that summer was Choral Conducting, given by G. Wallace Woodworth, director of the Harvard Glee Club. It was a large enough class to divide into a four-part chorus, which the participants took turns conducting. I was also the tennis professional for Harvard and the surrounding community. One of my pupils was the great ballerina/actress Vera Zorina. I couldn't get her to stop dancing long enough to get set for a stroke.

I spent the late summer in Lindsborg, Kansas, where my parents then lived. Harvard had asked me to remain and earn a doctorate, but I declined. The music department then recommended me for a choral-conductor job at a large university, but I declined that, too. It was a full-time, tenure-track position, and I wanted to have time to practice the piano, perfect my knowledge of score-reading, and compose what I could. I intended eventually to take the kind of job I had been offered, but only when I was ready.

5

DEVELOPMENT

While I was at Harvard I remained in touch with Harold Schmidt. In August he was asked by Menlo College to suggest someone to take over its music department the following month, and he recommended me. I accepted because it was a part-time job, and Menlo was only a couple of miles from Stanford. I was to conduct the glee club, lead a small band at football games, and coach the tennis team. I would receive room and board, fifty dollars a month, and whatever I earned by giving private piano lessons.

In September 1952 I took the train back to California. (I love trains.) Musically, all I had to show for the summer was the cycle *Three Madrigals* on poems of my father: "Impromptu," "Deny It as She Will," and "Moral Precept." I wrote the cycle at the end of the summer while visiting my parents in Lindsborg. The model for the first of these was a set of madrigals by Monteverdi that we had sung at Harvard. My father's text is adroitly madrigalesque:

Impromptu

A locust in the moon's spotlight,
Minstrel of the summer night,
Celebrates with rusty voice
Joys that locusts' hearts rejoice.
Blending cadence with the din,
A cricket, on his violin,
Seated in a stony grotto,

Saws a steady ostinato.

The second and third madrigals were harmonically influenced by Paul Hindemith's *Six Chansons*. This was a deliberate break with the Thompsonian style I had adopted at Harvard. Although I occasionally went back to that more conservative style in a few sacred works, I usually preferred a freer use of tonality. That could already be seen in the short pieces I wrote on Teasdale texts as a Stanford undergraduate, later to become part of *The Winds of May*. *Three Madrigals,* however, is a more ambitious set. Triadic harmony alternates with chords made up of major seconds and perfect fourths. As this cycle encompasses humor, love, and a more mature development of the texts, I consider it the first representative of my more characteristic style for secular choral music. I recently heard a fine performance by the Volti Chamber Choir and was pleasantly surprised by how well these pieces have held up after sixty years.

* * *

Menlo College in 1952 was a small, private, two-year school mainly for boys whose parents wanted them prepared for Stanford or UC–Berkeley. My first meeting with the glee club was not promising. I was greeted by a scraggly group of about fifteen boys lounging with feet up on desk chairs that had been turned around higgledy-piggledy. I found that the previous glee club had sung folk and popular songs in unison, with a few boys adding "harmony." It was a battle at first, but they finally learned to sing in parts. I had trouble finding interesting music that was easy enough for them, so I wrote arrangements (with piano) of three American folk songs: "Aunt Rhody," "Wayfaring Stranger," and "The Blue-Tail Fly." They require a good pianist, but the vocal lines are relatively easy. The young men responded well to the humorous, satirical texts of the outer pieces, and to the poignancy of "Wayfaring Stranger." Half the battle in winning over singers to new music is to find appealing texts. The three pieces were later published as op. 6, and the Royal Welsh Male Choir sang them on their 1965 tour of the United States and Canada.

The only good tenor in the Menlo group was Bob Shane, who later was a founder of the popular Kingston Trio. I appealed to the football coach to send me boys who needed an A to stay eligible and who could carry a tune. I promised to grade strictly on attendance. The glee club membership almost doubled, and I got one fine Samoan halfback/baritone, Al Harrington, later known as Ben in the original *Hawaii Five-O* series. I had no idea I was dealing with future pop celebrities.

I was at Menlo three years; after the first year I was hired by Stanford to be the assistant choral director, thanks to Harold Schmidt. With two part-time jobs and fairly steady work teaching tennis and piano privately, my days were full. My pupils were mostly eight- to twelve-year-old boys and girls from Woodside, an affluent neighborhood in the hills above Menlo Park where there were said to be more riding-horses than people.

Mornings, I often taught piano to children in their mansions; afternoons, I taught tennis to the same group on one of the families' private courts. The kids were bright and well-behaved, if you don't count occasionally teasing the teacher. After a piano lesson to an eleven-year-old boy, I said, "Let's do the Mozart for next week." He replied, "It's okay; *you* don't have to do it." When for some reason I asked the tennis group if they knew what "petite" meant, a visiting French student answered, "Yes, that's how Americans pronounce *petit.*"

At Stanford I rehearsed or sang with various choral groups. It was a thrill to be included in Schmidt's meeting with Bruno Walter at the San Francisco Opera House, where we rehearsed and performed the Brahms *Requiem*. The great German conductor was a soft-spoken man with a gentle smile but very sad eyes. Even Schmidt was impressed when Walter played the orchestral music from the full score (one that shows every player's part).

I was inspired, and ordered the complete set of solfège books from the Paris Conservatory in order to better learn the C-clefs. Many instruments—such as horns in F or clarinets in A—are written in one key but sound in another. The various C-clefs enable one to see, instantly and automatically, the actual note instead of the written one. Their use frees the conductor and composer from mentally transposing some instruments from one key to another. I sang the solfège exercises for many months before I had mastered the system. I supplemented it with score-reading exercises at the piano.

I was also determined to improve my piano technique. I took lessons from Herbert Nanney, the Stanford organist and excellent all-around musician. I practiced four or five hours a day in my little office facing the Menlo Commons. Unfortunately, the back of my office adjoined the locker room used by the San Francisco 49ers, who practiced on Menlo's field. Sometimes, after vigorous Hanon or Czerny exercises, I would hear a loud banging on the wall with a fierce admonition to "cut the crap." I switched to Bach or Brahms, but it usually failed to placate the angry warriors.

I must again remind the reader that even four or five hours a day of practice at the age of twenty-seven could never make up for the lack of steady practice as a child. How many times have I wished my arpeggios were as good as my backhand!

While working as Harold Schmidt's assistant, I was grateful that he programmed and allowed me to conduct my new compositions. The *Three Madrigals* I had written in Lindsborg were first sung publicly by the Stanford Madrigal Singers, with me in the bass section. I was neither a bass nor a tenor, but tried to fit in wherever I was needed. One Sunday I sang the *Messiah* with two different groups—in the afternoon as a tenor, in the evening as a bass.

The biggest stretch for me was singing tenor in the Brahms *Requiem* under Bruno Walter. For that performance we had two ringers in the tenor section who were permitted to skip all but the dress rehearsal: Jess Thomas (the future international Wagnerian) and a fellow named Ronnie White, who, at that stage, was just as good as Jess. Schmidt thought, quite mistakenly, that they might occasionally need a bit of help with entrances, so he put me between the two. What a glorious experience that was! I found myself fearlessly singing high-B-flats at full voice, knowing that these two powerful tenors would completely cover my puny efforts.

Each year Stanford invited a renowned American composer for a week's residency. The first was Henry Cowell. Harold Schmidt, ever my best promoter, asked Cowell to look over my *Three Madrigals*. He liked them well enough to recommend them to his publisher, Associated Music Publishers, an arm of G. Schirmer. That's how this group of madrigals became my op. 1. (Opus numbers traditionally reflect the order of publication, not of composition.)

Elliott Carter was Stanford's guest composer the next year. Among his duties was to moderate a concert of works by Stanford composers. It included the *Suite for Two Violins* I had written in Piston's class at Harvard, which I had revised and enlarged. When they were played, Carter said, "Well, I think we can all agree that we have just heard a very successful work." Encouragement like this is gold to a young composer, and you may be sure that I have remembered it verbatim. In retrospect, it seems a bit ironic that a mainstream, evolutionary composer like me owes so much to two of the icons of the American avant-garde.

Another five-movement work, *Suite for Piano*, op. 5, was written in 1954, after I had moved to Woodside (except for the scherzo, written as an undergraduate). Not very difficult (even I could play it), the piece did not have its professional premiere until my good friend Roy Bogas performed it in Berkeley around 1957; I dedicated it to him. It is one of those pieces that young composers write when they have more ideas than skill in working them out. (If Casper Boragine were still alive he would be nodding enthusiastically.)

My choral job at Stanford included singing in the choir every Sunday in Memorial Church. Romanesque in architecture, Byzantine in detail, with notable stained-glass windows and mosaics, its acoustics are spectacular for sacred choral music. Schmidt took full advantage of them with his excellent sixty-voice choir. As the church was interdenominational, we could sing the great choral works of every faith and nationality. There I made my first acquaintance with the Russians—Chesnokov, Bortniansky, and Grechaninov. In addition to singing two anthems every Sunday, we gave special concerts of larger works: the Bach B-minor Mass, cantatas by Mozart and Haydn, and the St. Nicolas cantata by Benjamin Britten, for which I conducted the smaller choir and its treble soloists—the two Schmidt children, Ann and Carl.

For the annual Spring Sing at Stanford in 1953, I wrote a motet for choir on a translated text from Euripides. I revised it in 1959 and gave it a text from Psalm 136 with the title "Give Thanks unto the Lord." This was the winning work in the S.A.I./C.F. Peters Inter-American Music Award for Vocal Music and helped put me on the choral map. It uses syncopation and double-choir effects, but harmonically looks back to my Harvard days.

* * *

The year 1955 was more notable for personal reasons than musical. I had often wondered what had become of that beautiful brunette I was so taken with at Harvard Summer School. Hoping her home address had not changed, I wrote her a Christmas card in 1954. About the middle of January I received a phone call from a woman who said, spookily, "This is a voice from your past."

I recognized Donata's voice immediately and replied, "Betty? Helen? Jane? Who is this anyway?"

"It's Doe Coletti!" And with some pique, she said, "I got your Christmas card."

She had graduated from Smith and had driven to San Francisco with a classmate. She didn't know for sure that I was in the area until her mother forwarded the card from Princeton. We got together, and I fell in love immediately. Doe is level-headed and totally honest, and she loves music with a passion. She has an excellent ear and discerning musical taste. She worked at Macy's when she first came to California, then as a clerk at KCBS radio. As my duties at Stanford had expanded to teaching harmony and conducting the opera that year, I finally had a decent income. We were married in Princeton on October 22, 1955.

Conducting the opera was my biggest job of the year. Opera at Stanford had always been a joint production of the music and drama departments, but the drama people decided they wanted to produce their own show in 1955 and hired me to be the conductor. This might have been an affront to the music department, which had produced the West Coast premieres of *The Rake's Progress* and *Peter Grimes*, among others. But the drama department wanted to perform an American opera, *The Golden Apple*, a musical adaptation of both the *Iliad* and the *Odyssey*, with music by Jerome Moross, lyrics by John Latouche. It's an opera in the sense that all the words are sung, but the music sounds more like Broadway. It had won the New York Drama Critics' Circle Award as best musical of 1954. The Stanford director wanted a conductor who (1) was versed in the idiom of American musicals and (2) would be part of the hired help.

That's what I was, all right, and I rebelled only on occasions when my rehearsal time was curtailed. I tried to make up for it by singing the cast's music to them during staging, but the director quickly put a stop to that. The show drew good crowds and reviews, but it was not very satisfying musically. Nevertheless, the experience it gave me rehearsing and conducting opera was a big step forward.

About the beginning of spring quarter, Harold Schmidt had a talk with me about my future. He pointed out that there would be no full-time jobs in the Stanford Music department for many years. He suggested that since I had held this part-time job for three years—one that was usually given to doctoral candidates for only two years at a time—I should think about the next step in my career. He strongly advised me to spend a year in Europe. Years later I learned that he already knew Harvard was considering me as a choral director and theory teacher, a position that would not open up until the following year. As some of my pianist friends were going to Vienna in the fall, Donata and I decided to spend a year there.

Doe spoke no German and what little I learned at Harvard was practically useless, so we took lessons that summer. We sailed in the first week of October, and then traveled by train to Vienna. Those first few weeks in the former imperial city were hardly glamorous.

6

VIENNA, *CON TUTTA FORZA*

Vienna was an occupied city until the year before we arrived. In early October 1956, it still looked much like a war zone. Anyone who has seen the classic film *The Third Man* knows what I mean. Donata hurt her back on the trip, and we could not attend a concert for several weeks.

Gradually, however, we got used to the dark, wet weather and found an apartment in the 18th District on *Aumannplatz*. A small park across the street had been the cemetery where Beethoven and Schubert were first buried. The rate of exchange was so staggeringly favorable to U.S. dollars that the one-bedroom apartment with living room, kitchen, and bath cost us only forty-five dollars a month. We later attended many concerts for less than fifty cents per ticket. But the apartment was not what one would expect in an American city. There was no hot water in the kitchen; we had to carry bucketsful from an overhead, hot-water heater in the bathroom to the kitchen sink in order to do dishes.

Our first concert was a performance of Bach's B-minor Mass in the *Musikverein* hall. At the opening sound of those two great "Kyrie Eleisons," we both broke into tears. Finally, this was why we were here.

On October 23 the Hungarian Revolution broke out. Within weeks, some two hundred thousand refugees fled, most of them across the border into Austria. Doe interrupted her *Deutsch für Ausländer* classes at Vienna University to work in one of the refugee camps at Traiskirchen. We saw and heard of many tragic cases of broken families, thwarted attempts to escape, and Soviet brutality. We got to know a refugee Hungarian violinist, nineteen-year-old Ulrich Kalmann, with whom I played sonatas. I dedicated the slow movement of my Piano Trio, op. 9, to Hungary: "Magyaroknak, 1956." The third movement begins with a rhapsodic violin solo in a style that I hope is reminiscent of Bartók.

I had begun the first movement in Woodside, but I wrote most of it in Vienna. It was my first large chamber work. I chose to begin with a piano trio for a good reason: I happened to know the pianist of a celebrated trio. Adolph Baller, a Palo Alto resident, had been an active pianist in Vienna before the Nazis tortured and deported him. He was the teacher of many of my pianist friends in the Bay Area, and later became a good friend and supporter of my music.

The Alma Trio was formed in 1942 at the Alma Estate of Yehudi Menuhin in Los Gatos, California (Baller had been Menuhin's friend and accompanist), and originally consisted of Baller, violinist Roman Totenberg, and cellist Gabor Rejto. I had heard many concerts by this remarkable ensemble, so the thrilling sound of a piano trio was well established in my ear. Of my chamber works, my Trio is still my personal favorite, and when I hear it I am taken back to those early days in Vienna when I was just feeling my way into becoming a composer. I am surprised now at how serious, even sad, much of it is, although there is youthful energy as well.

I did not compose much else in Vienna except to make some sketches for later pieces, and to compose most of the cycle *Four Songs for Baritone*, op. 10, on poems of my father: "The Green-blooded Fish," "July Rain," Inferiority Complex," and "A Farewell." I will write more about these songs later, when I discuss their performance by Theodor Uppman.

❉ ❉ ❉

That first year in Vienna was transformative. Mornings, I composed; afternoons, I studied and sometimes went to Doblinger's *Musikhaus*, where I could buy secondhand scores of symphonies and chamber music for a pittance. Almost every evening I went to a concert, reading a newly bought pocket score on the streetcar. You must understand that neither in Kansas nor at Stanford or Harvard did I have the time or money to attend concerts regularly. That was another hole in my musical development.

In Vienna at that time there were four orchestras, many chamber music groups, singers, pianists, violinists, touring ensembles, and soloists filling three opera houses, several concert halls, historic palaces, and private houses where special concerts were given, not to mention dozens of churches where complete masses of Mozart, Haydn, and Schubert were performed every Sunday with chorus and orchestra. All this took place in a city of one and a half million, about the population of present-day Phoenix. On one or two occasions I went to a church concert in the morning, a symphony in the afternoon, and an opera at night. When we took walks, I drove Doe crazy asking her to wait—sometimes in freezing temperatures—while I wrote down the concerts I saw announced on the advertising columns on the sidewalks. I didn't want to miss a thing. As we had no children yet, she attended most of these concerts with me.

I was not yet an opera fan, having attended only six or seven operas in my life. I had observed that American audiences "appreciated" opera more than they loved it. After all, it was nearly always in a foreign language. I hadn't fully realized that this was not how it was meant to be. In the eighteenth, nineteenth, and early twentieth centuries, when most of the standard operas were written, they were always sung in the language of the audience—except in English-speaking countries.

In 1957 Vienna, this was still true. The international star system did not become established until jet planes could speed divas from one continent to another overnight. Those divas couldn't be expected to learn every opera in Italian, German, French, Spanish, Russian, and English, so the practice of singing opera in its *original* language soon became the international norm. But the Vienna Opera until the 1960s was known as an "ensemble company." A permanent troupe of singers performed nearly all the operas—in German. Guest singers from elsewhere, with few exceptions, also had to sing in German.

In Vienna I worked hard to learn the language; before going to an opera I made sure that I understood every word. The first Mozart opera I heard in Vienna was not *Le Nozze di Figaro*, but *Die Hochzeit des Figaro,* performed in a small space in the *Redoutensaal* in the Hofburg Palace. There were few tourists in Vienna in those days, so the audience was almost entirely German-speaking. It was a revelation. Everyone laughed at the jokes and enjoyed all the stage business; there were no supertitles to watch. I finally understood what opera was all about. It was like our musical comedies except the music was continuous and much better. No wonder the Viennese are crazy about opera; it's their national pastime.

Only once before had I seen such love of opera. As an undergraduate at Stanford, I was one of several young men in our fraternity to be given seats occasionally at the San Francisco Opera by a former fraternity member, the retired general Philip Faymonville. He bought four subscriptions to every performance of every opera and gave all but his own to friends. The first time I met him, he invited three of us to have dinner at his house in the city, during which he told us all about the opera we were about to see: *La Boheme,* with Licia Albanese as Mimi. He had seen *Boheme* at least a hundred times, he said, and his enthusiasm kindled a great sense of anticipation in me, as I had not yet seen *any* opera. I was not disappointed, even though I did not always understand everything that was happening on stage. But I could feel the emotions of the characters powerfully through their music, which, together with the acting and beautiful sets, overwhelmed me. Eventually General Faymonville learned that I was a budding composer—I had improvised for him several times—and he advised me to start writing operas while I was still young. Although I did not heed his advice, the *Boheme* experience was a propitious one. I have never lost the conviction—reinforced in Vienna—that opera with compelling stories told through vivid music can be a popular art anywhere, even in the United States.

Here's a true story that happened in a small, suburban Viennese electric store. I sometimes bought the cheapest seats at the large *Staats oper.* They were cheap because you couldn't see the stage; you looked straight down on the orchestra. In front of these seats was a little shelf for a libretto or score, but there was no light. So I intended to follow the example of students—to buy a little battery-powered flashlight. I went to the small *Elektrogeschäft* in our neighborhood (almost every square block in Vienna then was a miniature village with all kinds of shops, none of them a franchise). I told the clerk what I wanted and why, and asked how large a light I would need without having to change batteries. "Well," he replied, "that depends on which opera you're seeing. This little light here will do fine for *Boheme* or *Capriccio,* but for *Carmen* or *Figaro,* you'll need this one. For Wagner, of course, or the original *Don Carlo,* you'll definitely need to change batteries at intermission." I bought the *Carmen* size, thanked him, and went on my way. Only later did the encounter strike me as exceptional. What would have been the answer to my request in a similar little shop in New York or San Francisco?

To live in a city so steeped in music deepened the feelings I already had about its importance. The reader already knows that music held a central place in my family as I grew up; to see that environment writ large in an entire city made me regret all the more how fractured and fragmented the music world had become.

I realize, of course, that even in 1957 Vienna, the musical life was no longer what it had been in that city's "golden age." In Mozart's time, everyone from the emperor to the bourgeoisie—with their servants— played music at home. Volkmar Braunbehrens, in his book *Mozart in Vienna* (1986), makes this observation:

"This constant activity among amateurs had one important effect on musical life: it created an insatiable demand for new compositions . . . and public concerts consisted almost exclusively of new music."

A twenty-first-century American critic might be tempted to use this as an argument for prodding our orchestras and opera companies to perform more new music, but that would overlook an essential truth: there is little demand for new music. The composers in Mozart's day spoke the same musical language as did those who heard and played their music. Today, especially in our universities and conservatories, there are hundreds of composers who, in effect, have no other audience but each other. This is a most regrettable consequence of pretending that music is a science.

Likewise, Braunbehrens points out that "in Mozart's time there was no clear demarcation between popular music and 'serious' music." The contrast with today's music world is again stark and sad: there seems now to be an unbridgeable cultural abyss between the popular and the "classical." It is a tragedy that so much serious music has already lost the common bond—its language—that it formerly shared with popular music. Consider Johann Strauss, Gershwin, the big-band orchestras of my youth—theirs were all forms of "popular" music solidly based on new incarnations of classic style. Today a rock or rap piece is so far from resembling a work by the classical avant-garde that it could be from a different planet.

* * *

Our time in Vienna was made much more pleasant by the company of colleagues from the Bay Area, all of whom became lifelong friends. Corrick and Norma Reddert Brown had been the piano accompanists for the Stanford chorus in my undergraduate days. They were studying piano at the Music Academy, though Corrick switched to the conducting class when he learned that he had been hired as the next conductor of the orchestra in Santa Rosa, his hometown. I had barely known the excellent pianists William Corbett-Jones and Sylvia Jenkins in the Bay Area, but we became better acquainted in Vienna. Bill has played many of my works. I had never met Roy Bogas before coming to Vienna, although he already had a reputation as a piano virtuoso. I first played my *Suite for Piano* for Roy in Vienna.

We also met a number of Viennese who became good friends. Ewald Winkler, a solo cellist in the Philharmonic, and his wife, the excellent violinist Christl Winkler, have been delightful hosts during our later trips to Vienna, and our very welcome guests in San Francisco. Felice Schediwy, a musical Californian married to a Viennese, had children the ages of ours and has remained a close friend.

* * *

Sometime in May I received an unexpected telegram from the Harvard music department, offering me a teaching and conducting position. If it had come at the *beginning* of my Vienna stay, I might have considered it. But now, flattering though it was, it took me only hours to send an answer. This was one of those "defining moments." I knew that I was deciding whether I would be a teacher and conductor, composing on the side—or a composer, teaching and conducting only as much as necessary. I declined Harvard's offer. A few friends and relatives thought I was crazy, pointing out how valuable the Harvard name would be in getting my works performed. But Doe supported me without question, and I have never doubted that I made the right decision.

Not only was I sure that I wanted to concentrate on composition, but I was also sure that I was not cut out to be a topflight choral conductor. The best people in that field have been singers or at least have studied singing extensively. I had never received more than minimal voice training nor felt that I had the expertise or the desire to teach amateurs how to sing beautifully. Not only that, but from the conducting I had already done, it was obvious that I lacked one attribute important for a professional conductor: an exceptional memory. From elementary school on, I did not memorize poems easily—not even those I liked—and it had been the same with music. To conduct even my own works I always needed the score. Donata remembers my music better than I do. I pride myself on being a good conductor; making that my life's work, however, would have been foolish.

I had additional reasons for declining Harvard's offer. With such eminent composers as Piston and Thompson on the faculty, it would have been difficult for me to find my own musical style. Moreover, I knew that Doe had come to California to escape the more rigid social hierarchy on the East Coast, where she had grown up. If we had returned to Harvard, there would have been pressure to adapt to the social life of her mother, her aunt, and other relatives in the East. Doe's mother came from a well-to-do family, some of whom had high social aspirations. She did not want any part of that, and neither did I.

We had intended to remain in Vienna through the summer, but had to return home for the June wedding of Doe's sister, Mimi, to Peter Dow. I was sorry not to be able to stay longer in Vienna. My German was just beginning to be fluent, and I felt at home in the city. It was a strikingly different life from any I had thought possible. I was determined to improve my German and return to Vienna. It took four years, but we did in fact return for an even longer time.

7

MAJOR / MINOR

Back in the Bay Area, we moved into a small house in a hilly section of Oakland called Montclair. The first piece I wrote in the little studio down the hill in our backyard was for Harold Schmidt: *Tourist Time: Five Satirical Choruses* for mixed chorus and piano, op. 11. About this time I began a relationship with E. C. Schirmer (ECS), the Boston music publisher that had been preeminent in the field of serious choral music for many years. ECS accepted the op. 2 motets and two other choral pieces, including *Tourist Time*.

The year 1958 was an important one: our first child, Katharine Whitney Mechem, was born on June 5. Doe developed an embolism a few days after bringing the baby home and was readmitted to the hospital. The doctor told me she could die. Doe's mother came out to help me look after the baby. Doe recovered after several weeks, but it was a harrowing time for us all. When we finally returned to something like normal, I wrote an unaccompanied choral piece, "The Protest of Job," adapting a text from the book of Job. Our troubles in no way matched those of the biblical Job, but they at least made me understand those tragic words. As I read them now, I can see that I set them as if they were a conversation between my father and mother, the atheist and the devout.

> *Mixed Chorus:* Wherefore is light given to him that is in misery, and life unto the bitter in soul? Why is light given to a man whose way is hid, whom God hath hedged in? Let the day perish wherein I was

born! For the thing which I fear cometh unto me. I am not at ease; neither am I quiet; neither have I rest.

Women: Is not the fear of God thy confidence, and thy hope the integrity of thy ways?

Mixed Chorus: There is hope of a tree that it will sprout again; through the scent of water it will bud, and put forth boughs like a plant. But man dieth, and wasteth away. As the river decayeth and drieth up, man dieth and wasteth away. And thou destroyeth the hope of man.

Women: O thou that tearest thyself in anger: shall the earth be forsaken for thee?

Mixed Chorus: Have pity upon me, O ye, my friends.

Later in 1958 I began to write a cantata called *Songs of Wisdom* that would include "The Protest of Job." It is a thirty-three-minute work: essentially five motets on Old Testament texts, alternating with quasi-plainsong recitatives from Ecclesiastes, each for one of four soloists. This was my most ambitious work so far; I conceived it as a search for the meaning of life. Brahms's *A German Requiem* was a model for the personal and wide-ranging use of biblical texts. *Songs of Wisdom* has never enjoyed great popularity, however. I'm afraid that a long, serious, and rather difficult unaccompanied sacred piece without any liturgical focus will never have a wide sale. This became a recurrent problem throughout my career. I couldn't resist setting powerful, large-scale texts that do not fit easily into choral programs, church services, or budgets.

Nevertheless, *Songs of Wisdom* makes a strong impact in performance, and the good reviews and response from conductors and singers have supported my belief in it. Charles Susskind, in the *Berkeley Daily Gazette*, declared it "a mature work, grandly conceived and admirably executed in a wholly original fashion that bears no discernible allegiance to any 'school' of composition, and that resembles (in format) nothing so much as opera. . . . The young composer's irrepressible spirits might well find full expression in a comic opera that . . . could become, at long last, *the* American folk opera."

I find it startling that a man I'd never met knew twenty years before I did that I should have been writing operas.

✧ ✧ ✧

I stated in the prelude that I do not share my mother's religious beliefs; indeed, I am not a believer in the doctrine of any particular faith. Why, then, have I chosen biblical texts for some of my choral pieces? Because they are great poetry on universal truths. Nearly all religions have certain fundamental humanitarian beliefs in common, and I do not think the doctrinal differences are as important as the philosophical similarities. They all speak to our better nature, to what we instinctively know is right. Where the Bible uses the specific words "God" or "the Lord," to me those mean "Love" or "the human spirit." As I have grown up in the Judeo-Christian tradition, I also respond *emotionally* to the poetry of the Bible. Not only have I heard those texts in church with my mother, but I have also heard and sung the great music of Palestrina, Bach, Handel, and Brahms that they inspired.

Also in 1958, I began to compose what eventually became the finale of my First Symphony. This was a "Holiday Overture"; its frequent meter changes and cross rhythms in a very fast tempo required intensive rehearsal. Later, when Josef Krips gave the premiere of the symphony, one of the players said of the finale, "This wasn't the music Krips grew up with. He had us play it over and over until we had taught it to him." There's only a grain of truth in that, however, as Krips and the San Francisco Symphony gave a spirited performance of the complete work. It was in 1959 that I decided the overture would be more effective as the final movement of a symphony. I called the movement "Theme and Derivations," a title I had used first for the third movement of my Woodwind Trio—but more about the symphony later.

Living in the East Bay, I renewed my friendship with the pianist Roy Bogas, who lived in Berkeley. He and his wife held regular chamber music readings at their house. A number of players from the San Francisco Symphony took part, among them flutist Lloyd Gowan. My *Divertimento* for Quartet of Flute and Strings, op. 12, was first tried out by Lloyd and other friends in 1958. It was written rather quickly as a piece of *Gebrauchsmusik*, but it became my most popular chamber work. Some pieces come easily and turn out well; others are difficult to write and turn out badly. But the reverse is also true.

There doesn't seem to be any relationship between how hard a piece is to write and its quality. *John Brown*, my most ambitious opera, posed enormous compositional problems but is probably my best work. I can think of choral pieces that I wrote in one or two days: some are good, some not so good; ditto those I struggled over. When I wrote the *Three Madrigals*, op. 1, in Lindsborg, I complained to my father that I would never be a professional composer because it took so long to write a piece. He told me not to worry: "The more you write, the faster it will come and the better it will be." In general, he was right.

In 1958 I began to take viola lessons from a friend in the symphony. String instruments are the backbone of the orchestra and of many chamber ensembles, but their technique is difficult to understand for composers who do not play a string instrument. I never got beyond the ability to play the easier Mozart quartets, but I have continued to study string technique and bowing all my life, and have taken Sandor Salgo's advice always to indicate the bowings for each new work. After a premiere, I study the string parts, trying to understand the bowing changes players have made. I advise young composers to learn to play a stringed instrument.

Donata had taken violin lessons for a short time as a child and resumed study in 1959. She is very musical, but her experience as a choral singer had not prepared her for the more complicated rhythms in instrumental music. To help her over this difficulty, I wrote *Ten Easy Violin Duets*, op. 15, for her and her teacher. All ten can be played in first position, and each deals with some unusual aspect of rhythm or meter.

✻ ✻ ✻

Dmitri Shostakovich and other Soviet musicians visited San Francisco in November 1959 as part of a goodwill tour sponsored by the U.S. State Department. I was invited to the reception and was thrilled to meet the great Russian composer. Sitting in his appointed place, he looked even more dour and solemn than his photographs, if that is possible. And why wouldn't he? Harassed by his government, forced to make this trip with Soviet *apparatchiks*, it must have been torture for the shy, reclusive genius. I tried through the interpreter (KGB no doubt) to open a discussion with him, but I didn't get much further than I had with Joe Louis. Donata told him that his Fifth was the first modern symphony she really liked, but the word "modern" was left out of the translation, and Shostakovich was quite annoyed that someone would try to butter him up with such an outrageous claim.

✻ ✻ ✻

By that time I had a modest, growing catalog of works, and was eager for my music to be performed in public. The only venue open to new music in the Bay Area then was the Composers Forum, administered by composers in the music department of the University of California at Berkeley. I submitted several works at various times: the Piano Trio, the newly published *Three Madrigals*, the Woodwind Trio, *Four Songs for Baritone*, and others. I never received responses to my submissions, and I had a hard time even getting the scores back.

Those who know the history of musical composition in postwar academia will have no difficulty understanding why the work of a tonal composer—whether good or bad—was held in contempt by many writers of atonal music, which was *de rigueur* at UC–Berkeley and at many other universities and conservatories. Someone like me just didn't get it; it was as if I were a Holocaust denier or a flat-earth freak. They wrote articles describing people like me as "mugwumps" and "ultraconservatives." As a liberal-minded free-thinker, I found it all hard to take.

(I hasten to add that the UC–Berkeley music department has also included many distinguished writers and scholars—Joseph Kerman and Richard Taruskin, to name only two—whom I have greatly respected. And some of the composers there, such as Andrew Imbrie and Leon Kirchner, were excellent, serious musicians. As former students of Roger Sessions, however, they had a very different outlook on new music than I did.)

About that time, I was reading a biography of Handel and noted that when he came to London to live, he introduced himself with a public concert of his music. I decided to follow his example in San Francisco. I persuaded the program director of the Museum of Modern Art to allow me to present a concert of my music in its theater without cost, under the auspices of the museum. Harold Schmidt agreed to bring his Stanford Choir to sing the premiere of *Songs of Wisdom*, and insisted that I conduct it. Roy Bogas enlisted two of his friends from the symphony to join him in presenting the Piano Trio, and players from the symphony gave the first public performance of the Woodwind Trio. Filling out the program was the premiere of *Four Songs for Baritone* with James Standard, accompanied by Bogas.

I put up posters in San Francisco, Berkeley, and Oakland, and rehearsed the musicians. The museum director told me they had never sponsored one-man shows, even for visual artists, and as no one could remember a one-composer concert in San Francisco, I had the good fortune of presenting a novelty. The audience would hear music for strings, winds, piano, solo voice, and chorus. All this made publicity easier to come by. The concert was given March 10, 1960, in the theater of the old Museum of Modern Art next door to the opera house. We had a good crowd, including all the local critics.

The reviews from the local papers and from *Musical America* were excellent. Arthur Bloomfield, writing in the latter magazine, praised the "high level of imaginative musical quality throughout the evening." I later found these reviews a great help in getting further performances, even of larger works. But I did hear from a colleague at UC–Berkeley that my "hubris" had put some noses there out of joint. I replied that I had tried the Composers Forum repeatedly; if its directors had not ignored me, I would never have gone to the trouble of producing my own concert.

One immediate benefit of the museum concert came from Berkeley (not the university). A private group of musicians and music lovers had established the Amphion Concert Foundation with the goal of sponsoring an annual concert by a promising young musician. After hearing my San Francisco concert, they chose "The Choral Music of Kirke Mechem" to be their presentation the following year. They asked the Stanford Choir to repeat *Songs of Wisdom* and to sing a group of motets and madrigals; Harold Schmidt brought his smaller Stanford Chorale to perform the latter. The concert was given February 28, 1961, in the Berkeley Little Theater.

The year 1961 also saw the premiere of my first commissioned orchestral work, *Haydn's Return: Fugue and Variations on the Farewell Symphony*, on February 14. The commission came from the Santa Rosa (CA) Symphony, conducted by my old friend Corrick Brown. As the local *Press-Democrat* described it, "A fugue and six variations on thematic material from the Haydn symphony ingeniously bring the players back onto the stage and into the music until not only the original Haydn orchestra is employed, but eventually the entire instrumentation of the modern symphony."

Our second daughter, Elizabeth Celia Mechem, was born July 1, 1960. It was an easier birth, without complications, and Doe was able to join me for the July 29 recital by Theodor Uppman at Stanford. The program included the *Four Songs for Baritone* on poems by my father, which I had begun in Vienna in 1957. Ted had sung the title role in the premiere of *Billy Budd* at the request of Benjamin Britten, and was a leading baritone at the Metropolitan Opera. With Ted's permission, I dedicated my song cycle to him. He later sang it on tour, but I believe this was his first public performance of the cycle. Roy Bogas came down from Berkeley to accompany him. There is an unusual story behind the text of the first song.

G. K. Chesterton, the esteemed British author, published a literary magazine to which my father subscribed. Chesterton suggested that a newspaper headline he had read—"A Green-blooded Fish Has Been Found in the Sea"—would make a good refrain for a ballade, a strict verse form in which the word "Prince" nearly always begins the final quatrain. My father took him up on it, and the poem appeared in *G. K.'s Weekly*.

It is difficult to say where the other poems first appeared. My father's poems were published mostly between 1925 and 1960 in magazines and newspapers: *The Nation, The New Republic, Harper's, The Saturday Evening Post, Life, The Kansas Magazine, The Kansas City Star,* and others. He later reworked nearly all of them, often destroying the originals and with them the records of first publication; some were also given new titles. For his ninetieth birthday I had a small anthology published of what I considered his best poems. Called *I Could Hear the Least Bird Sing*, it included the poems used in *Four Songs for Baritone*.

Like the first poem, the last was based on an antique verse form, this time the French *rondeau quatrain*. Each new verse begins by repeating, in a regular pattern, a line of a previous verse. I was intrigued by this and set out to see if I could use the same repeats in the vocal line, sometimes changing its octave or accompaniment.

A Farewell

Before it was spring
And I was a man,
I gave you my heart,
As only youth can.

I gave you my heart,
Naive as a youth,
Believing love beauty

And beauty all truth.

As only youth can,
    I swore I was blest,
With love like a shadow
    Clasped to my breast.

With love like a shadow
    Grotesque on the pyre
Where youth burned to ashes
    With lust for the fire.

Clasped to my breast
    No more!—nor Farewell;
And may we meet never
    This side of hell.

I was surprised by how well this formal design worked musically; it gave the song a unique shape. But the critic for the *Palo Alto Times* singled out "July Rain" as "the most impressive," and noted that the performance was marked by a strange event. First, here's the poem, a sonnet:

July Rain

There is a ghostly autumn haunts July
When summer nights give way to drifting mists
And breezes freshen in the foggy sky
And the melancholy moon floats where she lists:
The inexplicable season, full of sadness,
Of premonitions, of unreasoning sorrow,
That strike a terror at the heart of gladness
With vague forebodings of the unborn morrow.
The shadows fall now over the sunny days
Of unseen figures, dark with all the vain
Wild questionings that mournful autumn lays
On the despairing heart. Now with the rain
Falls this strange time of sighs and nameless fears
That catch the throat and fill the eyes with tears.

The strange event noted by the reviewer, and by many listeners in the hall that July afternoon, was this: when Uppman began this song it started to rain—and stopped shortly after the song ended. For readers who do not live in the Bay Area, I must explain that here in the summer it never—but *never*—rains.

By the end of February 1961, it had been nearly four years since we left Vienna. I never lost the determination to return. I had been studying German with Mrs. Erna Straus, a German Jew who had escaped the Holocaust. I went to her apartment in Berkeley for two hours every Monday afternoon; we spoke no English. I read both volumes of *Faust* and many other German and Austrian classics with her. She was an inspiring woman of about seventy, a grandmother, and a music lover, and we talked of many things. My regular visits to her felt something like going to church every week. I always left in a more peaceful, elevated frame of mind than I had brought with me. I dedicated Symphony No. 1 to Erna Straus.

* * *

We had decided to leave for Vienna at the end of March. The Amphion Foundation had commissioned me to write a substantial work for voices and instruments; this would help pay for the trip. Real estate prices in the Bay Area had already jumped sufficiently for us to receive a good monthly rent from our Montclair house, and the exchange rate in Austria still made Americans seem rich. Our house in the Oakland hills was idyllic in some ways. It was quiet; Doe could stroll with the children along a path through the woods, and we had a spectacular view of the bay. What was lacking was proximity to cultural and social life. I felt isolated. The musical events in the East Bay were dominated by UC–Berkeley. I longed to connect with the great musical heritage of Vienna again, a city where I could thrive in a stimulating and supportive environment.

I had worked hard these four years in Oakland—too hard, as it turned out. During the second year I began to have frequent headaches of increasing intensity. I probably would not have gone to a doctor had not a first cousin died at age twenty-nine from a brain aneurism preceded by headaches. None of the tests my doctor gave me showed any problem.

"What are you doing for relaxation?" Dr. Wilbur asked.

"Not much," I admitted.

"Why don't you make more time to do something you love, like listening to music?"

I didn't know whether to laugh or cry. It had not occurred to him that a person who spends day and night writing, studying, practicing, and thinking music can hardly *relax* by listening to it. I explained this to him.

"Do you still play tennis?"

"No, I gave that up years ago."

"Well, I think that's your problem, Kirke. Start playing again, just for the fun of it. Anyone who has been an athlete all his life can't suddenly go without aerobic exercise. Your headaches are telling you something important."

I heeded his advice and have done so ever since. The headaches disappeared. Several years later, when we lived near Golden Gate Park in San Francisco, I played tennis regularly. Rosie Casals—later to win many doubles championships with Billie Jean King—was only about seventeen when I often played with her. A few years later, when she and Billie Jean were in town, I played doubles with them—an honor I remember with pleasure. Billie Jean, as everyone knows, later became a spokesperson for women's rights. My impression of her was simply as a wonderful tennis player with a quick smile and a generous attitude.

8

VIENNA, RECAPITULATION

The ride into Vienna from the airport showed a bleak, gray city still in the grip of winter, even though it was the first of April. The rooms in our pension were cold; when we asked for heat, we were given the astounding news that in Vienna the heat is turned off April 1.

The Eichmann trial was being followed around the world, and the seventeen-year-old daughter of our landlord was concerned that Eichmann would not receive a fair trial. When we mentioned some of the atrocities he was accused of, she replied, "Well, the Jews did some terrible things in Vienna. They cut down a tree on our street."

It was several weeks before I found a place to live; it was in a superb location. We shared an apartment at *Schubertring* 8 across from the *Stadtpark*, a few minutes' walk to the principal concert halls, the opera, and *Akademietheater*. Our quarters were at the rear of the apartment, but the location made up for a lot. The apartment was owned by a Hungarian woman, Vera Hochner, whose fifteen-year-old son, Robert, grew up to be one of Austria's most respected television commentators. His mother was far from a satisfactory landlady, but she knew many people in the Viennese music world. She introduced me to H. C. Robbins Landon, who later did me the favor of recommending a good music copyist.

I soon began attending the daily concerts of the International Society for Contemporary Music. Each year, ISCM presents its World Music Days Festival, hosted by one of ISCM's member cities. This year it was Vienna's turn. The goal was "to provide a feast of contemporary music across a broad range of contemporary practice." I was eager to hear these new pieces from around the world, and attended every concert for thirty days. But the "broad range of contemporary practice" was limited to experimental and atonal music; I never found a piece I liked. Hearing these concerts in the great musical city of Vienna was like attending a play in Esperanto on Broadway—Vienna took little notice of them.

My first task was to find a text for the Amphion commission. At the *Amerikahaus* library I discovered a charming tale in the Apocrypha of the Bible, from the book of 1 Esdras. It was one of the most popular tales of antiquity; it related King Darius's contest to name the strongest force on earth. The contestants—his three young guards—declare in turn: "Wine" (sung by a tipsy baritone); "The King" (a stentorian bass); and "Women" (a lyrical tenor sings their praise). I decided to have each soloist supported by a different instrumental sound—a wind quintet for the baritone, a grand piano for the king, and a string quintet for the tenor. As the soloists compete against one another, so do the instrumental groups. A mezzo soprano is the narrator. The chorus acts as a kind of grand jury, questioning, disputing, and helping the narrator tell the story. The tenor, Zorobabel, the advocate for women, wins the contest—after all, it's sex that makes the world go round. But then he turns to the crowd and declares that there is a power stronger than all these things: truth. Without truth, all else is wicked.

I wrote in the program note, "Although the biblical story is often deliberately naïve or told with tongue in cheek, it makes its point dramatically, with wit and charm. The music aims at nothing loftier than conveying these qualities." In those days it was necessary to apologize for wit and charm.

A few years later, when I made revisions after the premiere, I changed the title from *Zorobabel* to *The King's Contest*, op. 42. I'll say more about the checkered history of this piece in a later chapter. As you can tell from the description above, this is getting pretty close to opera. It has never been staged, but a few productions—with costumes and minimal acting—have recognized its dramatic possibilities. Nevertheless, I doubt that there is enough suspense or plot for this to succeed as a one-act opera, except in a semi-staged concert performance.

* * *

A month after we moved into the *Schubertring* apartment, President Kennedy met with Soviet premier Nikita Khrushchev in what was called the Vienna Summit, June 3 and 4, 1961. On the second day (the day our Lizzy took her first step) I walked over to the site of the meeting to see if I could catch a glimpse of the two most powerful men in the world. I waited outside. Before long, Khrushchev strolled out smiling and serene, surrounded by a few undemonstrative aides. A few minutes later, when an agitated Kennedy appeared, the contrast was striking. All the way to his car he gesticulated and talked quickly to his aides. I walked home and told Doe it didn't look good for the United States. Our government at first tried to portray the meeting as a diplomatic triumph, but two years later Kennedy said, "He beat the hell out of me." That's more like it, I thought.

✵ ✵ ✵

When our year's contract for *Schubertring* was up, we moved to *Modenapark* 3, where we had a larger, newer apartment all to ourselves. I rented a vacant room nearby in *Reisnerstraße*, where I could work without the household distractions. Both were within easy walking distance to concert halls; I attended almost as many concerts as I had four years before.

One concert that I well remember involved Benjamin Britten, who accompanied a recital of his songs by his partner, the tenor Peter Pears. I was especially struck by *Seven Michelangelo Sonnets*. I attended the concert with a British friend, who introduced me to Britten after the concert. He was sitting down, signing autographs. When I was introduced as a visiting American composer, Britten rose, shook my hand, graciously answered my questions, and asked about my own work. I had long admired his music and went home happily invigorated.

The Beethoven symphony cycle that Josef Krips conducted stands out in my memory, too, not only for the excellence of the performances, but also because I had a chance to speak with him after a concert. He was one of the great Viennese conductors of the day, internationally known, and was to play an important part in my future musical life.

I was still not as interested in opera as in chamber and orchestral music. But I vividly remember seeing *Die Meistersinger* for the first time and being overwhelmed by its beauty and mastery. I became acquainted with three operas by Richard Strauss that I had not known before: *Arabella, Intermezzo,* and *Capriccio.* I particularly liked *Capric-*

cio, but *Rosenkavalier* remains my favorite—so beautiful, humorous, and fancifully *alt-Wien*.

By now I knew enough German to enjoy going to plays. A Viennese friend taught me to understand even the droll humor of the idiosyncratic Viennese playwright Johann Nestroy. I attended more plays than I did operas. If you are surprised that a composer should express such a preference, please note that the same was true of Brahms. Yes, I know that Vienna is famous for its music, but the United States also has superb orchestras, choruses, and soloists. Our country did not, however (except perhaps for Broadway), have the great tradition of theater that Vienna is famous for in the German-speaking world. I love theater and regularly attended professional productions in the Bay Area. Nearly always, however, the lesser parts (and sometimes the larger ones) were played by actors with little talent or training. In the many productions I saw in Vienna, there was never a role too small to be played by an excellent professional actor.

The first music I wrote in my *Reisnerstraße* "studio" was a set of three wild pieces for mixed chorus and piano called *Im Lande des Morgensterns, op. 21 (In the Land of Morgenstern)*. The texts were by Christian Morgenstern, a German poet who specialized in nonsensical humorous verses—something like Ogden Nash, but much darker. Here is no. 2 of my set, *Die Geruchsorgel* ("The Odor Organ"), with my version for singing it in English.

Palmström baut sich ein Geruchs-Orgel	Palmstrom built himself an odor-organ
und spielt drauf von Korfs Nieswurz-Sonate.	and played von Korf's Sneezewort Sonata.
Diese beginnt mit Alpenkräuter-Triolen	This piece begins with eucalyptus triplets
und erfreut durch eine Akazien-Arie.	and enchants us with a catalpa aria.
Doch im Scherzo, plötzlich und unerwartet,	In the scherzo, swiftly and unexpected,
zwischen Tuberosen und Eukalyptus,	there between the roses and coreopsis,
folgen die drei berühmten Nieswurz-Stellen,	suddenly come the three notorious sneezeworts
welche der Sonate den Namen geben.	from which this sonata derives its title.
Palmström fällt bei diesen Ha-Cis-Synkopen	Palmstrom tries to play these wild syncopations
jedesmal beinahe vom Sessel, während	but almost falls off the organ; meanwhile
Korf daheim, am sichern Schreibtisch sitzend,	Korf, safe at home, goes right on composing
wirft Opus hinter Opus aufs Papier.	opus after opus after opus.

The music stretches tonality and choral convention. Years later, a conductor writing a doctoral dissertation on my choral music was so befuddled by it that he asked me to help him analyze *In the Land of Morgen-stern*. Here is part of my reply:

> In general, don't try to find established musical forms to fit these into. They are crazy poems, and the music is a little crazy, too. You can certainly find standard devices such as fugal episodes, augmenta-tion and ostinatos, but I doubt that you'll discover any hidden sonata, rondo or any other forms of that kind. The pieces are mostly episod-ic. . . .
>
> Sometimes a purely musical analysis misses the point. Humor in music is a risky business (especially in translation), and explaining it is even riskier. But I think you could say that these are among my first attempts at the kind of musical parody that has drawn attention in *Tartuffe*. In "*Die Geruchsorgel*," in fact, some of it is parody of opera.
>
> I need to tell you also that in "*Die Geruchsorgel*," the high point of the "Sneezewort Sonata" occurs when Palmstrom tries to play the "wild syncopations" and falls off the organ [or piano bench]. I've seen performances where the accompanist did this literally and the audi-ence didn't stop laughing for a full minute. . . . One more "insider" detail: the dedication of no. 3, "The Lattice Fence," is to my son, who was born in Vienna on the day I finished this piece, December 14, 1962.

That was a special day, indeed. After Donata had an easy delivery, I received a phone call from the doctor: "*Herr Mechem, Sie haben einen Sohn!*" The hospital was the old *Frauenhospiz* on *Peterjordanstrasse*, across from *Türkenschanzpark*. I arrived at the hospital before they were ready for me, so I went to a *Gasthaus* next door and ordered a beer for everyone in the house; we all drank a *Prosit!* to Edward Joseph Mechem. He did not become an architect, as I thought he might; he became a computer expert. That's a blessing— he has been the reason I can write this on an iMac instead of on a typewriter.

✲ ✲ ✲

Because I heard so much chamber music in Vienna, I was inspired to compose a string quartet. I heard and studied the Beethoven quar-tets, and many by Haydn, Mozart, Dvorak, Bartók, Debussy, and Ravel. I composed String Quartet no. 1, op. 20, on *Reisnerstrasse*, completing it on March 24, 1963. I copied it myself and sent the score to the *Prix de Composition Musicale Prince Rainier III de Monaco,* an international competition with a distinguished jury headed by Nadia Boulanger. To my great surprise, my quartet was the only American entry to win anything: it was runner-up in the chamber music category. A bonus to this good fortune was that a small story appeared about it in one of the leading Viennese papers. I had been told that Josef Krips was an avid newspaper reader, so I sent him a note, asking if he would look at my First Symphony. Unbeknown to me, he had just accepted the post of conductor of the San Francisco Symphony Orchestra, and he answered my note immediately. He asked me to leave the score for him at the Imperial Hotel. By the time I could do so, however, he had gone on a long tour. Still, this connection to him became valuable to me later in San Francisco.

The quartet is a twenty-minute work in three movements, dedicated to the Marin Arts Quartet, San Francisco Symphony players who lived in the North Bay. They gave the first performance. It has been recorded by the Czech Quartet, who played it on tour, and by the New Zürich Quartet for the Swiss Broadcasting Corporation. It is not atonal, but I consciously explored a wider harmonic range than I had used before. I think the last movement is a bit too long as written, and I have offered some optional cuts, which the Swiss players used. Oddly enough, most colleagues and audiences liked this piece better than I did until recently. (I had to grow into it, I guess.) It's not so lyrical as the Piano Trio, and the slow movement has elements of a tragedy, which makes me uncomfortable.

We had been in Vienna now for well over two years and decided it was time to go home. We were tired of being foreigners. We knew that we did not want to return to the house in Montclair. The convenience of having almost everything within walking distance in Vienna persuaded us to look for a house in a residential district of San Francisco, close to schools and shopping, and within easy streetcar access to cultural events. On July 3, 1963, two days after Lizzy's third birthday, we took a train from the Westbahnhof to Rotterdam. As we disembarked at the train station, we had so many suitcases, boxes, and toys that people asked if we were refugees.

Doe and the children spent two months in Massachusetts with Doe's sister, while I went on to California to sell the Montclair house and buy one in San Francisco. Proving once again that it's better to be born lucky than smart, the house in Montclair had almost doubled in price.

We were able to make a down payment on a big, run-down, but well-constructed house in the Forest Hill section of San Francisco, where we still live.

9

CHORAL CYCLES

The next eight years—described in the following five chapters—included some of the best and a few of the worst years of my musical life. Aside from a disruption caused by a traumatic event in our family, there was a steady rise in my productivity and number of performances, followed by institutional and cultural changes that led to falling spirits and fewer compositions.

Fortunately, I received a commission shortly after settling into our house in San Francisco. For its seventy-fifth anniversary, Wheelock College, a women's school in Boston, asked me to compose an accompanied choral work based on texts by women. I looked at hundreds of poems until I found a few that seemed to go together. Then I realized that they formed a story of a woman who falls in love with the wrong man. (Opera manqué?)

The result was *The Winged Joy: A Love Story in Seven Parts*, op. 22 for women's chorus and piano. The form of the work is unusual. The number of voices decreases from four to one as the protagonist moves through progressive emotional stages: (1) the fullness of love, (2) betrayal, (3) cynicism, (4) resignation. But as she gradually recovers her self-esteem and good spirits, the number of parts increases one by one to four again: (5) rejection of the returned suitor, (6) reawakening to the beauty of the world, (7) lighthearted mocking of the game of love. The use of a solo mezzo-soprano in no. 2 is balanced by the same solo voice in no. 6. There are also melodic motifs that recur from movement to movement—most obviously the sea-chanteys in no. 2 (a quodlibet), which return in no. 7 (the unfaithful lover was a sailor). Throughout the cycle there are juxtapositions of major and minor, reflecting the ambiguity in young love—the mercurial interplay between happiness and unhappiness.

The performance history of *The Winged Joy* is as unusual as its form. I was not able to attend the premiere in Boston on February 21, 1965. When I was in that city several years later, however, the conductor let me hear a recording of the performance—with his profound apologies. I had obviously overestimated the skill of the Wheelock singers. Music was not a major subject at the college and my piece was too difficult. But when the first performance of a new work is a bad one, I am inclined to blame myself. By the time I heard the recording, the work had already been published, and I had written it off as a failure. A composer should never let a piece be published before hearing it; I regretted making an exception in this case.

It wasn't until 1973 that I heard the cycle again. I was in my hotel room in Kansas City for the American Choral Directors Association's national convention when I had a call from the Women's Choir of the University of North Carolina at Greensboro. The conductor, Richard Cox, was performing *The Winged Joy* for the convention, and invited me to hear a rehearsal. This was news to me, and I came to the rehearsal with some apprehension. What I heard was a gift; it was as if these musicians had presented me with a delightful new piece! From that moment, I have considered *The Winged Joy* to be one of my best choral pieces, and have had the pleasure of hearing it sung by some of the best women's groups in the country.

* * *

Donata had sung rounds, catches, and canons all her life; I had not, but she made me an enthusiast of the genre. She and I and her sister, Mimi Dow, sang many of those that I wrote and later collected into a volume called *Epigrams and Epitaphs*, op. 13; they are unaccompanied and meant only for informal use, though hundreds of copies were sold to young choruses as humorous introductions to contrapuntal singing. The later *Catch 22 (and 21 Other Catches and Canons)*, op. 50, has optional piano accompaniments and concert endings; the set was premiered in 1986 by the Collegiate Choir, Illinois Wesleyan University, under David Nott. Those from both volumes were written in hotels, airports, the houses of hosts and hostesses—anywhere an occasion presented itself. I have great fun writing these little puzzles that circulate from singer to singer—it's like telling an intricate joke—though some do have serious texts.

Skipping ahead four decades, the most recent volume in this genre is *Birthdays: Round Numbers*, op. 72. The titles are: "Bridget at Ten," "Turning Twenty," "Is Thirty Young?" "Forty Notes for Forty Years," "Fiftieth Birthday Card," "Advice on Turning Sixty," and "Is Seventy Old?" Each number began as a round; I later developed them into a cycle for mixed chorus and piano. It is more adapted to concert use than are the other collections. Most of the texts I wrote myself:

> Though twenty's a time to feel frisky,
> The road you have taken is risky.
> It's bumpy and gritty
> And leads without pity
> To forty and fifty and sixty.

The second day of the year 1964 was auspicious. I received in the mail a note from Joseph Krips, new conductor of the San Francisco Symphony, to whom I had sent my First Symphony. I was shocked by its first words, "Just to cut the matter short. . . ." *Oh Lord, he never wants to hear from me again!* But the note went on to say that the orchestra would perform my symphony next season! Krips's English was good but not perfect; when I looked up his first phrase in a Viennese dictionary of American-Austrian conversational style, I found that "just to cut the matter short" was mistakenly translated with the inoffensive German expression meaning simply "to be brief." Krips had obviously bought the same book I had.

In 1964 I composed two more choral cycles—*Five Centuries of Spring* and *Seven Joys of Christmas*. The cycle is a form that greatly appeals to me. As in *The Winged Joy*, it gives the composer a chance to tell a story through diverse poems. Dr. Donald Miller, in the *American Choral Review*, claimed that I acted like a librettist nearly every time I wrote for chorus.

There is a practical advantage to the cycle: conductors have the flexibility of performing either separate pieces or the entire set. In preparing for the premiere of *Songs of Wisdom*, Harold Schmidt's Stanford Choir performed each of the five movements as a separate motet for Sunday services over a period of two months. A further advantage of the choral cycle is that it involves both audience and singers in the text to a greater extent than does the usual succession of unrelated three-minute pieces. Even if the cycle does not tell a story, the poems are related in some way, and there is often musical continuity as well. I elaborated on this in an article, "The Choral Cycle," which I wrote for the March 1970 issue of the *Choral Journal.*

Five Centuries of Spring, op. 23, is a madrigal cycle that uses poems about spring by representative authors from the sixteenth to twentieth centuries: Nash, Shakespeare, Blake, Housman, and Millay. My music incorporates some characteristics of the musical style of each century: harmonic cross-relations and irregular rhythms for the sixteenth; long, melodic, imitative lines for Shakespeare's Sonnet 98; triadic melodies, rapid imitation, and sequential development for the eighteenth century; the predominance of melody supported by rich harmony for the nineteenth. Millay's poem, "Spring," is bitter and mocking. I chose it as appropriate for that twentieth-century music that denied beauty and celebrated dissonance. Accordingly, the music for the finale mocks all that came before, ending with an insane travesty of the birdcalls from the first piece.

It should be apparent to the reader that I do not regard today's choral groups as capable only of "pretty" music or of traditional religious settings. A large body of choral music in nineteenth-century Germany was justly denigrated as *Kapellmeistermusik*—works by conductor-composers who knew how to make a choir sound beautiful, unsullied by any original ideas. That kind of choral composer is still with us, but that is only one side of choral music in America today.

Thousands of excellent choral groups—professional, community, university, even the better school and children's choirs—demand and get new music of substance. No orchestra or opera company commissions the number of compositions that many choral groups do. The number of skillful, imaginative composers for chorus—from tonal to avant-garde, some of them conductors—has increased with the rapid expansion of choral singing in this country. Not only is this a healthy phenomenon musically, but it benefits our society, too.

Choral music is today what art songs (lieder) were in the nineteenth century—a genre where musical amateurs can thrive. Before electronic media made us passive listeners, classical music was sung and played at home to a degree that most people today can hardly fathom. Instead of a television set, a piano was the center of the living room in millions of homes, not only in Europe but also in the United States. There was a huge audience of musical amateurs who knew these songs from the inside (as they did symphonies through popular four-hand piano arrangements). As Hans Gal wrote in his 1961 biography of Brahms, "The impoverishment of present-day music continues progressively and ceaselessly, for neither radios nor record players can be true substitutes. Anyone who has ever taken part, no matter how humbly, in the joy of making music will understand this. Only those who experience music through active participation can truly make it their own." It is choral music that is chiefly responsible for keeping this tradition alive.

Chorus America recently published a study that found that in 2009, more than forty-two million adults and children regularly sing in choruses. Among the characteristics of adult choral singers when compared to nonsingers are "higher levels of civic involvement." Young singers (ten million) "are better participants in group activities and have better emotional expression; singing enhances their memory skills, self-discipline, social development, and academic success," according to the educators and parents surveyed. Every choral director has witnessed many a troubled youngster's life turned around by singing in a chorus. And I am only one of many thousands who met their spouses in a chorus. Under a good conductor, singers not only learn to read music, they perform great works by a variety of composers. They learn to work together; they encounter great poetry, foreign languages, and other religions; they travel to distant cities and continents. I have worked with public high school choruses (Napa High School under Travis Rogers, for instance) whose singers are of such high quality that they regularly receive music scholarships to leading universities. If the mayors of our cities knew the social power of choral singing, they would sponsor a chorus in every neighborhood.

❊ ❊ ❊

Living in San Francisco was expensive, and we no longer had the rental income from our house in Oakland. I had been looking for a part-time teaching job for months, when a full-time appointment for one year fell into my lap. In late August 1964, San Francisco College for Women suddenly needed someone to teach theory and to conduct the Chamber Singers for one year. That title in most colleges denotes the most expert choral group, so I planned a rather difficult Christmas program. A week before the first rehearsal, I held auditions. To my dismay, all who came were freshmen, and only one had ever sung in a chorus before.

I scrapped my original program. I knew that I could write easy pieces for this group faster than I could search the literature and order copies from publishers. If chromatic notes and difficult leaps are kept to a minimum, anyone who can carry a tune can sing in parts. Even difficult rhythms can be learned by beginners. To create arrangements of carols was an obvious solution—but not the department-store carols!—and I wanted to write more than simple chordal arrangements. When I decided on *Seven Joys of Christmas*, I looked for carols from different countries that would express seven joys of the season: love, bells, Mary, children, the New Year, dance, and song. I wrote one piece a day; the a cappella cycle was ready for the first rehearsal.

Before the work was published, I added a light keyboard accompaniment and also made an arrangement for mixed chorus. Later, at Roger Wagner's request, I added a version with chamber orchestra; still later I made an accompaniment for solo harp. Wagner and Robert Shaw were at that time the best-known choral conductors in the country. It was a boost to my career when Roger performed *Seven Joys* regularly at Christmas time with the Los Angeles Master Chorale and orchestra, and took the unaccompanied version on tour with his smaller chorale.

A half-century after the cycle was written, its publisher, ECS, issued a special anniversary edition of the orchestral score. A few years earlier, the publisher's recording company, Arsis, had produced a compact disc of all my Christmas choral music: *Seven Joys of Christmas and Beyond.* It was sung by the Stanford University Chamber Chorale and Orchestra under the excellent direction of Stephen M. Sano in the glorious acoustic of Stanford's Memorial Church.

For a work with such humble, utilitarian origins, it has had remarkable success with groups of all kinds, from children's choirs to symphony orchestras. It doesn't hurt that Christmas rolls around every year.

10

SINFONIA GIUBILANTE

Finally, on January 6, 1965, I heard Josef Krips conduct the San Francisco Symphony Orchestra in the premiere of my First Symphony. It was the first new piece Krips had performed in the city, and it was the most significant musical event in my life so far. To tell the truth, when I received that acceptance note from Krips a year before, I quickly looked over my score to see if it was, in fact, good enough for this honor. I had written it several years earlier and was afraid it would be a flop. I remember groaning to Donata, "This isn't as good as I can do now! Should I tell Krips that I'll write a better one for him to play instead?" As usual, she calmed me down, and pointed out that I had often doubted my works before they were performed. It was a mere case of "first-night jitters."

Today, premieres of new music are common, but in San Francisco at that time, this would be the first major premiere in several years, and the newspapers gave it extensive publicity. Alfred Frankenstein, at the end of his long tenure as chief critic of the *San Francisco Chronicle*, asked me to write an article about the symphony and about myself for the Sunday edition before the premiere. That should have made me even more nervous, but by that time I had heard the first rehearsal and was astounded that my piece sounded so good! (Other composers have told me similar stories about the first time they heard a top-flight orchestra play their new work and found themselves wondering, *Did I really write that?*)

Here is a shortened and slightly edited excerpt from the article I wrote for the Sunday *Chronicle*. Warning: You will see how the brash composer—still smarting from the rejections of the new-music establishment—compounded the resentment that he had aroused five years earlier by producing his own concert.

✿ ✿ ✿

The professional musician flouts the listener at his peril. The attitude which this betrays can become suicidal, and has already contributed greatly to the present-day alienation of composers from the public. The question may arise: what public and which composers? I mean only the public that goes to classical concerts because music gives them something worth the effort and expense. And I mean only the composers who address themselves to this public.

And so if I say that even in art, the customer is always right, I hope you will not think I mean that if the Beatles fan doesn't like Beethoven, it's Beethoven's fault, or that if every classical-music lover doesn't understand a new work on first hearing, it is necessarily a bad piece. One must always make allowance, on the one hand, for lack of listening experience or musical sensitivity and, on the other hand, for genius that occasionally may startle more than please—to say nothing of individual taste.

But after a long period of time, assuming sufficient exposure, you can't blame the music public for not taking this or that composer to its heart. And if I have pretended that serious music is a commodity, let me add that its "consumer"—that subtle combination of human soul, brain, emotions, and ear which we call "the music lover"—is a good deal more complicated, demanding, and worthy of our consideration than we composers often acknowledge. We are, in fact, created in the music lover's image; in the beginning was the listener.

Of course no self-respecting composer writes music according to such concepts of supply and demand. We write what we like, as the saying goes. But how much that cliché leaves unsaid! Composers are subject to the same self-deceits, hidden motives, ambitions, and contradictions that make living the non-definable process it is. So a composer writes what he or she *is* —this says a little more, but not much. And some "creative" people—I use quotation marks to salute the word's current pretentious usage—claim that they create for no audience at all, only for themselves. That may be true, but their work is then self-therapy and will only accidentally be art. And their avowed noncommunication itself communicates something.

The word communication is popular now in art criticism. It is the key word in discussing the previously mentioned rift between the artist and the layman. And it has the advantage of being equally handy in music, literature, and the visual arts. I think it is all to the good if it helps us get back to the analogy of music and language.

It is true that this comparison was vastly overworked in the nineteenth century. Eventually, with the help of detailed programmatic pieces, it was distorted to the point where some writers believed all music could be translated into words, in spite of the embarrassing fact that the translations never agreed. It was only a short step from this to the grotesque notion that music was simply emotion imprecisely stated. Here the reaction had to set in.

Now that we have had about a half-century of the reaction—beginning with the seemingly inoffensive doctrine that music is nothing more than "organized sound"—we have come to equally grotesque notions. We have tried out all sorts of ways to do this organizing, believing that one sound was as good as another, and one system of organization as good as any other system. It was just a matter of understanding it, getting used to it, getting rid of old habits of hearing.

But music is not an arbitrary system which can be replaced at will by any other system. It is not a system in the scientific sense at all—it is truly a *language* . It is subject to the same law of general comprehensibility as the spoken word. Its subject matter is not only emotion, but thought, and it is in its own terms just as precise as a spoken language is, perhaps more so. We composers work as hard to give an idea its exactly proper expression as a poet does—an A-flat will not do where a G is wanted.

Its vocabulary is not static, but, as with any language, is constantly changing, not only through daily usage, but also through the imaginative treatment of artists. As with a spoken language, this process has been slowly evolving for centuries.

Logic plays a smaller role in this evolution than does intuition. What seems right and makes its way into traditional usage *is* right. What seems wrong is not accepted, no matter how good its credentials. It is just as idle to berate a music lover for not understanding some new "system" of composition as it would be to blame an English-speaking person for not understanding the word "nrsthcn," explaining that it is the logical grouping—backwards—of all the consonants of the German "nichts" and the French "rien," meaning nothing.

And it wouldn't help if you claimed that this was a new, truly international language devised to wipe out the old, decadent system of nationalistic misunderstandings which have been at the root of the world's suffering, blah, blah, blah. One might appreciate your ideals, might say your new language was very "original" and "interesting," and if the listener were very foolish, he might even blame *himself* for not understanding a word you said.

If all this seems like a roundabout way to prepare readers to hear my symphony this week, it is because I don't think they need any preparation other than being sensitive to music. You will find no analytic notes in the program because I haven't written any. It should be enough to know that the work is in three movements: a long, free sonata form, a short intermezzo, and a "Theme and Derivations," a title intended to describe a playful combination of rondo, variation, and free development.

Although I usually avoid describing what my music "sounds like," perhaps I can honor the desperate need some people have to fit every composer into a pigeonhole by divulging the "school" to which I belong, namely, the neo-Baroque-Classic-Romantic-Modern-Avant-Traditional-Imaginists. (You may not have heard of our movement, since we remain fiercely underground.)

But let me warn you: even if you happen to favor this particular school yourself, I give no guarantee that you will like my symphony. All I can say is that I liked it when I wrote it five years ago. Since we agreed earlier that a composer writes what he is, perhaps you have some idea what to expect now that you have read some of my pontifications. But don't be too sure. As we have all sadly learned, composers nowadays are devilishly clever at talking a better piece than they have composed.

✿ ✿ ✿

As a matter of fact, I still believe today most of what I wrote in that article half a century ago, but I have learned to show more respect to those with differing views. I may not like atonal or gimmicky concert music any better now than I did then, but I recognize that there are no "authoritative" verdicts on the value of a new work. We composers all write the best music we can, music that we ourselves like. But that doesn't mean audiences have an obligation to like any of it, or that orchestras or opera companies have a responsibility to perform any that *they* don't like—including mine. Nor do I expect atonal composers to like my music any better than I do theirs. Some composers aim for the larger music public, others for a specialized audience.

Many excellent, smaller ensembles that champion advanced music—not necessarily atonal—have dedicated audiences. In San Francisco, the Kronos Quartet has made an international name for itself by playing offbeat works, many of them interesting and some even with a bit of humor. Volti is another such group in San Francisco; it specializes in modern choral music, some "interesting" and some that is *really* interesting. All over the western world there are concerts and festivals of contemporary music, and many have loyal supporters. These audiences find offbeat music exciting and original. Such audiences are not, by and large, made up of the general music public. But every major metropolitan area counts its population in the millions, so even a niche group can be quite sizeable. But who's counting?

Throughout the twentieth century it was assumed by its more hardcore partisans that if atonal music were heard repeatedly, it would begin to sound like Mozart. Yet most efforts to "educate" audiences and make them feel their "responsibility to the art of our times" were counterproductive. It was—and still is—a mistake to market new music as badtasting medicine that's good for you.

These partisans were also fond of claiming that only ugly art reflected the reality of the horrendous historical era in which we lived. But art can be more than a mirror. It is a puny art that cannot rise above its environment and try also to inspire, console, delight, and show the better way. Mozart put it this way: "Passions, whether violent or not, must never be expressed to the point of exciting disgust, and music, even in the most terrible situations, must never offend the ear" (letter to his father, 1782, translation by Emily Anderson). Let us never forget that for many people, beauty is what makes life worth living. As Nietzsche wrote, "Without music, life would be a mistake."

The value of new music is a complicated issue, and I will come back to it later. But my *San Francisco Chronicle* article did rattle the cage of the new-music community, and I later had to pay for that audacity. Some friends called me brave—others, foolish.

The premiere of the First Symphony was a greater success with the audience than I had dared hope, and all the reviews were positive. Even Frankenstein was heavy on the praise and light on the constructive criticism. Winthrop Sergeant, then music critic for the *New Yorker*, wrote me that if even a "dyed-in-the-wool propagandist" for atonal music like Frankenstein praised my work, I had achieved a remarkable success.

The symphony intentionally looked back to the classics. In the first movement I wanted to see what I could do with the large-scale, free sonata form that had been the basis of so many great symphonic movements of the past. Was it still possible to be creative—with modern tonality—in such a traditional form? Hearing the symphony now, I see that the "Theme and Derivations" of the finale is more original than the first movement, and more characteristic of my personality and later work.

After the fourth performance Krips commissioned me to write a Second Symphony.

11

LENTO, MOLTO SOSTENUTO

The success of the First Symphony brought with it many benefits, not the least of which were further performances of the work, increased interest from publishers, and more performances of my other music. Several other orchestras played the symphony in the next couple of seasons, but I was disappointed that none of the major orchestras were interested. I was beginning to learn a hard truth: for contemporary music, most orchestras don't want secondhand goods. It is hard enough for them to sell tickets for new music even with the glitter of a "world premiere," and they can't risk offering previously owned vehicles. That attitude has become self-defeating: the public hears only the new, un-tried music—rarely the few successes—and new music becomes ever harder to sell.

My good friend William Corbett-Jones, who had taken over the job of pianist for the Alma Trio from his former teacher, Adolph Baller, asked me to write a work for him—it became the Piano Sonata, op. 26. It is quite different from the jazzy, nostalgic Suite for Piano, op. 5; this probably explains why some listeners prefer the earlier one. In its more dissonant style and rhetorical content, the sonata is more like the String Quartet than any of my other works. I began it in the last month of 1964 and finished it early in 1965. Corbett-Jones gave the premiere at the San Francisco Conservatory of Music on April 27, 1965, and recorded it for Sonic Arts. I like the last movement best, but the critic for the *Musical Times* of London dismissed its "toccata-style finale" as "of less

distinction" than the "neo-Romantic, occasionally even Brahmsian powerful first movement."

The *Chronicle*'s new chief critic, Robert Commanday, formerly of
the UC–Berkeley faculty, was surprisingly kind, calling it "a work of
vitality and fresh ideas, venturing farther into the land of asymmetric
rhythms and dissonance than his earlier works." But then he added, "a
weak sister of a second theme and a hullabaloo final cadence are faulty,"
and declared that the sonata needed a fourth movement. Commanday
always tried to be fair, and he was a positive force for music in the Bay
Area. We composers cannot expect every critic to share our point of
view or taste, and we cannot complain about these differences if we are
treated with respect, as I was by Commanday. On the other hand, I
would be lying if I pretended that I was not upset by another kind of
criticism—that born of personal antagonism (which is rare, thankfully).
The "fair" kind is hard enough to take sometimes; the hostile sort is
maddening. We composers want our reviews to be written by our moth-
ers.

The summer of 1965 had been taken up with minor revisions of the
First Symphony and with preparing for publication the scores and parts
of the works going to E. C. Schirmer, the Boston publisher, which had
offered to publish all my works. At the end of August, I began a part-
time job teaching two harmony classes at San Francisco State University. I was not prepared for the work load. At the College for Women I
had no more than five or six students in each class; at the state university there were about forty. Harmony is a discipline best learned
through exercises written and corrected daily. This turned out to be
full-time work at half-time pay.

✼ ✼ ✼

The year 1966 is remembered with sadness. In March our youngest
child, Jennifer Coletti Mechem—born June 3, 1964—came down with
spinal meningitis and lost her hearing. We were told by an eminent
specialist that it was folly to expect any of it to return, but a second
opinion gave us hope. In fact, after a few weeks, she did begin to hear
faintly in one ear. With a powerful hearing aid she has been able to live
an almost-normal life—except that music makes little sense to her. Fortunately, she was a very bright, outgoing child, who at twenty months
already had a vocabulary of about 350 words. Doe was urged by the
hearing clinic to spend hours every day reading and talking with her to

make sure she could build upon the language she already had. She attended regular schools and universities, has married, and has two beautiful daughters.

The premiere of the Second Symphony had been announced for March of the coming season, so I had only six months to compose and copy the work. Krips and the orchestra gave four excellent performances, beginning March 29, 1967. The first movement was long and lyrical—too long—with a great variety of development and contrasting material. For the second movement, I developed and expanded an andante grazioso, "Theme and Variations," based on the slow movement of my Divertimento for Flute and Strings. One of the variations introduced a *lento, molto sostenuto* section that arose from the grief and love I felt for my youngest daughter. The third and final movement was more like a scherzo and, because I had so little time, I also borrowed from a previous work, this time writing a quodlibet based on two movements of *The Winged Joy*. You may remember that the texts of those two movements had to do with a fickle sailor and included several sea chanteys. Again, I did not write any program notes for the symphony, but I should have, at least for the last movement.

I was not as happy with the work as I had been after hearing the First Symphony, and neither were some of the critics. Krips, on the other hand, told reporters that the Second was far superior to the First. My own view was that the third movement was really a scherzo, and that I should add a real finale. Krips agreed and told me, "Add a fourth movement, and I'll play the symphony again in two years." I also wanted to shorten the first movement and to tighten both of the other movements, which needed lighter instrumentation in places. I could see that I had worked too quickly. I therefore devoted nearly all my spare time the next year to revising and recopying the Second Symphony. (Remember, this was before computers; the copying of scores and parts all had to be done by hand.)

An important digression was one of my own favorite choral pieces, *The Shepherd and His Love*, op. 30, composed as a wedding present for Carl and Betsey Schmidt. Carl is the son of Harold Schmidt; both he and Betsey were finishing their doctoral studies at Harvard, where the premiere took place. Harold conducted the Harvard Summer School Chorus in Sanders Theater; the bride and groom were members of the chorus. It is an eight-minute piece for a six-part chorus, piccolo, viola, and piano. The men sing the words of Christopher Marlowe's "The Passionate Shepherd to His Love"; the women respond with Sir Walter Raleigh's rejoinder, "The Nymph's Reply." The *Choral Journal's* "Chamber Music" editor wrote, "This is the type of writing which may well be the salvation of choral music . . . a constantly changing fabric of sound. . . . You owe it to yourself as an inquisitive musician to look at it." The young reviewer for the *Harvard Crimson* called it "an exercise in corn."

My love of theater led me in 1967 to the American Conservatory Theater's production of Molière's *Tartuffe*. It was the first offering of ACT's first season in San Francisco. In the brilliant Richard Wilbur translation, with William Ball's stylized, almost-choreographic direction, it seemed to me like a comic opera waiting for the music. I looked over my copy of the play, looked for ways to cut and rearrange the scenes for an opera, and went back to another performance. I was not yet ready to write an opera, but I kept my notes for the future.

In the fall of that year I returned to Lone Mountain College—San Francisco College for Women had become coeducational and had changed its name—this time as composer-in-residence. The college became part of the University of San Francisco; through all its name changes it had served as USF's music department.

Krips and the San Francisco Symphony premiered the revised version of Symphony no. 2 on January 15, 1969. The four movements were now listed as Sonata, Quodlibet, Canzona *con Variazioni,* and Rondo. This time I wrote a note for the symphony program in which I told the story of the second movement, about the young woman and the sailor who abandoned her. The response of the audience to the new version of the symphony was considerably more enthusiastic than it had been to the original—I was brought out for four curtain calls. This was certainly in part because of the rhythmic new finale, which gave an intricate, brightly orchestrated, and upbeat ending to the symphony. The reviews were still somewhat mixed, although this time they included a 100 percent rave and a 100 percent vilification—emblematic of how polarized the world of new music had become.

Krips was again my best supporter. He recommended the Second Symphony to the New York Philharmonic, to be included in a program he was to conduct the following season. The performance never materialized, but I was nonetheless grateful for his confidence in me.

12

UNRESOLVED DISSONANCE

There were gathering clouds after the premiere of the Second Symphony. Krips would be leaving; Seiji Ozawa had been hired to replace him the following season. Attempts to interest Ozawa in my music went nowhere. I was also disturbed that critics were more and more influenced by the trend toward atonal and experimental music. The same music that had been praised a few years ago was now categorized as "conventional" or "old-fashioned" (the very words that J. S. Bach's sons used for their father's music, and that the Wagnerites used against Brahms).

I went about the business of composing, although I didn't feel like tackling anything big for a while. In 1969, at the request of brass players in the San Francisco Symphony, I transcribed *Whims* for brass quintet, calling it *Brass Buttons*, op. 32b, for children's concerts. I dedicated a song cycle for mezzo soprano and piano, *Goodbye, Farewell and Adieu: Three Songs of Parting*, op. 33, to three different mezzos: Carolyn Reyer, Shirley Verrett, and Margery Tede. The third song, "Let It Be Forgotten," was based on the choral piece I wrote at Stanford. At the request of E. C. Schirmer, I composed *Two Christmas Ballads,* op. 35, for chorus with guitar accompaniment, on poignant poems by Sara Teasdale and Phyllis McGinley; later I added an optional accompaniment for keyboard.

In 1970 I had a chance to do something big again, and in a quite different style. I received a commission from the Elgin (IL) Choral Union to compose a cantata for chorus and instruments to celebrate the chorus's twenty-fifth anniversary. Hanging in my studio for many years was a small, framed poster with the words of William Byrd's "Preface" to his 1588 *Psalms, Sonnets & Songs of Sadness and Piety*. It had been given to me by Harold Schmidt, and I had long believed it would be an ideal text for choral music.

Reasons briefely set downe by th' author, to perswade every one to learne to sing:

First, it is a knowledge easely taught, and quickly learned, where there is a good Master and an apt Scholler.

2. The exercise of singing is delightfull to Nature, and good to preserve the health of Man.

3. It doth strengthen all parts of the brest, and doth open the pipes.

4. It is a singular good remedie for a stutting and stamering in the speech.

5. It is the best meanes to procure a perfect pronounciation, and to make a good Orator.

6. It is the onely way to know where Nature hath bestowed the benefit of a good voyce: which guift is so rare, as there is not one among a thousand, that hath it: and in many that excellent guift is lost, because they want Art to expresse Nature.

7. There is not any Musicke of Instruments whatsoever, comparable to that which is made of the voyces of Men, where the voyces are good, and the same well sorted and ordered.

8. The better the voyce is, the meeter it is to honour and serve God there-with: and the voyce of man is chiefly to bee imployed to that ende.

Omnis spiritus laudet Dominum.

Since singing is so good a thing, I wish all men would learne to sing.

My twenty-six-minute cantata is called *Singing Is So Good a Thing: An Elizabethan Recreation*, op. 36. While I made no attempt to stay within the Renaissance style, except in one or two short passages, I consciously tried to evoke it by characteristic uses of melody, rhythm, and harmony. The instruments were chosen in the same spirit; they are modern equivalents of those that were common in Byrd's day.

The work is divided into twelve movements, the choral sections alternating with instrumental dances of the period. In some cases, a dance introduces the raw material upon which the chorus that follows is based. Each of the twelve pieces represents a form in common use during the Renaissance: praeludium, corranto, canzonet, gigg, and so forth.

The cantata is one of my favorites, probably because I had always loved singing Elizabethan madrigals. It has had excellent reviews and many performances. Perhaps its most persuasive tribute came from the people who had commissioned it. Twenty-five years later, the Elgin Choral Union commissioned me to compose a work for its *fiftieth* anniversary, which will be discussed in chapter 18.

Singing Is So Good a Thing was published by C. F. Peters. For those perceptive readers who may wonder why this piece was not published by E. C. Schirmer, with whom I had an exclusive agreement, I must explain that I ended my contract with ECS in 1971. For the next nine years I published with Boosey & Hawkes, Carl Fischer, C. F. Peters, and Theodore Presser before publishing exclusively with G. Schirmer from 1980 to the present.

The break with ECS was necessary because the new president was ignoring the terms of our contract. He was annoyed that I insisted, after several years of waiting, that he do what we had agreed upon. Out of the blue, he returned to me all my works that ECS had not yet published. When I did not respond for several months, he offered to take them back, but I had already found interest from other publishers, and had decided I wanted no more to do with that particular individual. It turned out to be for the best, but it was a painful decision. I was suddenly in the position of starting all over again with my largest, most difficult pieces—symphonies and cantatas—the ones that meant the most to me. This was a serious problem, and it added to two other recent musical disappointments: the realization that the San Francisco Symphony was now closed to me; and the local critics' increasing condescension toward my "conservative" music. (I've never been a conservative; I'm a conservationist.) I found myself looking for greener grass on the other side of the Atlantic.

(E. C. Schirmer was later sold; for the next thirty-five years it was run by an excellent and helpful team under Robert Schuneman, who restored the company to its former quality and integrity.)

✿ ✿ ✿

I had liked England and its people immensely during the war, and had the wholly unfounded idea that it was more impervious to musical fads than brash, young America. After all, Britten and Walton were not exactly revolutionaries, particularly when compared to Ives, Babbitt, and Cage, who were being celebrated here. In my state of despair and disconnect, I thought that London might be a good place for me. We could get a good rental income from our house, and I had three new commissions. I had nearly completed two of them; why not finish them in London, which was cheaper than San Francisco anyway?

We rented out our house and flew to England the first week in September 1971.

Kirke Mechem, age 5, Topeka, KS. From the collection of the author.

Corporal Mechem, U.S. Army, England, 1945. From the collection of the author.

Kirke Field Mechem, the composer's father. From the collection of the author.

Katharine Lewis Mechem, the composer's mother. From the collection of the author.

Kirke Mechem. Tennis publicity photo, Stanford University Department of Athletics.

Harold Schmidt, Stanford University choral director. From Fabian Bachrach.

Wedding photo, Kirke Mechem and Donata Coletti Mechem, Princeton, NJ, 1955. From the collection of the author.

San Francisco Museum of Art poster, 1960: "Music of Kirke Mechem." From the collection of the author.

Conductor Josef Krips and Kirke Mechem, 1969, San Francisco Opera House before the premiere of Mechem's Symphony No. 2. From Ed Schwartz.

Evelyn de la Rosa and John Del Carlo in the world premiere of *Tartuffe*, San Francisco Opera, 1980. From Tony Plewick, San Francisco Opera Magazine.

Montage from the Russian magazine *Kavkaza*, honoring an all-Mechem concert by the USSR Radio/Television Orchestra, March 30, 1991. From Murad Kazhlaev.

Mechem family photo, Christmas 1996. Back row: Kirke, Donata. Front row: Edward, Elizabeth, Katharine, Jennifer. From the collection of the author.

Kirke Mechem conducts "Las Americas Unidas," 1986, for international telecast. From the collection of the author.

Kirke Mechem, St. Petersburg, Russia, 1996, for the Russian-language premiere of *Tartuffe*. From the Moussorgsky National Theater for Opera and Ballet.

Harrietta Krips and Kirke Mechem, Vienna, 2002, for the Austrian premiere of *Tartuffe*. St. Stephen's Cathedral in background. From the collection of the author.

Interview at Mechem concert in Moscow, 1991. Left to right: Kirke Mechem, Donata Mechem, Murad Kazhlayev, Corrick Brown, Irina Arkhipova. Face not visible: Katharine Mechem. From the collection of the author.

James Maddalena and Donnie Ray Albert in Lyric Opera Kansas City's world premiere of *John Brown*, 2008. From Douglas Hamer for Lyric Opera Kansas City.

Robert Orth, Diane Lane, and Christopher Burchett in Skylight Music Theatre's world premiere of *The Rivals*, Milwaukee, 2011. From Mark Frohna for Skylight Opera.

13

LONDON

Deceptive Cadence

We rented a townhouse on Porchester Terrace in the Bayswater section of London. It was like a vertical apartment, narrow and high. First I put the finishing touches on two of the commissioned pieces: *The Children of David*, op. 37, for Schola Cantorum of Palo Alto, and "Praise Him, Sun and Moon," op. 38, no. 1, for Whittier College's European tour.

The Children of David: Five Modern Psalms is an ambitious twenty-six-minute cantata for mixed chorus and organ, with a mezzo-soprano solo in the second and fourth pieces. The title refers to the later poets who carried on the tradition of David, the pre-Christian psalmist. In my notes, I described these as "psalms to the spirit of life, with recurring musical and poetic motifs." The poems are "Psalm" by Carol Dinklage (a friend from Harvard); "Joy" by Robinson Jeffers; "The Song of David" by Christopher Smart; "Man of My Own People (The Jew to Jesus)" by Florence Kiper Frank; and "Pied Beauty" by Gerard Manley Hopkins.

The premiere drew excellent reviews. However, the work requires a fairly large chorus and a first-rate organist and organ, so it is not often performed. It straddles the line between sacred and secular—was I once again trying to reconcile the philosophical views of my mother and father?—and it is too difficult for all but the best church choirs. Even

The American Organist's review—"these poignant words are galvanized into high drama, and the music exudes emotion"—couldn't help.

You might think I would have learned something from my experience with *Songs of Wisdom*—namely, that extended choral works that do not fit any holiday or liturgy are a hard sell. But these are great humanitarian poems that I set in dialogue with one another, and I gave them some of my strongest music. I like to think that serious choral directors will discover them yet. Are not spiritual, secular ideas still valued? Universities still teach these ideas. *The Children of David* pieces are craggy and bold, and do not find favor with those who want "pretty" music, with the exception, of course, of works by dead composers. (I'm getting there as fast as I can.)

The commissioned work I had not yet begun to compose was for the Varsity Bards, the University of North Dakota Men's Chorus, Roger Wilhelm, Director. As I had just arrived in England with three daughters (and a son), I intended to write a cycle called *English Girls*, op. 39. I looked for English poems that would be appropriate to each girl. "Jenny Kissed Me" by Leigh Hunt was perfect for Jennifer. Ben Jonson's "Come, My Celia" from *Volpone* fit Elizabeth, whose middle name is Celia. I couldn't find a match that I liked for Katharine, so I chose a poem by Robert Herrick, "On Julia's Voice," that fit her quiet, thoughtful personality, and that served as a contrast between the lively outer pieces.

* * *

Before I left San Francisco, Joseph Scafidi, manager of our symphony orchestra, had kindly written a letter introducing me to orchestra managers in London. He suggested that I should first visit John Dennison, general manager of the Royal Festival Hall on the South Bank, where all four of London's orchestras performed at that time. I made an appointment with Dennison, who patiently and sympathetically explained the situation of English orchestras in regard to contemporary music. He told me that these orchestras were heavily subsidized by the government through the Arts Council, and in return, 20 percent of the music they performed must have been written by living British composers. "Frankly," he said, "that is already more contemporary music than the public wants to hear."

This news should have brought me down to earth in a hurry. But I clung to the harebrained hope that if I could convince one of the major

English music publishers to take me on, perhaps I could stay there, become a citizen, and take advantage of that handsome government subsidy. You can surely detect my desperation, grasping at straws so slender. But after all, I reasoned, a mutual friend had written me a warm letter of introduction to Alan Frank, head of the Music Department of Oxford University Press, and I could offer him two symphonies with excellent reviews and several chamber and choral works.

Mr. Frank received me cordially, introduced me to William Walton, who happened to be in the office that day, and Frank and I had a friendly talk about my career and intentions. He asked me to leave my scores and other material with him and to come back in two weeks. I was greatly encouraged, and returned at the appointed time, full of hope.

Unfortunately, this castle in the air collapsed, too. I was told by Frank that he and his editors thought my music was excellent, but that it was not what they were looking for at the time. When we met, he said, he had thought I was much younger than I was (story of my life). He said that my music was similar in style to what they already published in Walton and others. What they wanted now was not an established composer who was already published by a number of good firms, but a young composer on the brink of an important career in a newer style—someone whose name would then be associated with Oxford Press for many years, each work helping to publicize the others. As an example, he mentioned a young, twelve-tone composer who was just beginning to be known. (I haven't heard of him since.)

This was a blow. I took my scores and walked home across Hyde Park. At the age of forty-six it seemed that my career had run its course. I was too old! I sat down on a bench and fought off tears. I was so disheartened, I wrote nothing more in England than a full orchestration of *The King's Contest*. All thought of remaining in England for more than a year was gone.

But I couldn't give up. I had planned a trip to the United States in January to attend the premieres of *The Children of David* in Palo Alto and *Singing Is So Good a Thing* near Chicago. On the way home I would stop in Syracuse, New York, for a three-day residency at Onondaga College, where I would lecture and conduct my own works. I wrote to Boosey & Hawkes in New York and arranged a January meeting with the head of that office, Stuart Pope. I explained in my letter what had happened to my relationship with ECS, and reminded him that he had invited me to resubmit the First Symphony if the situation changed. In a following phone conversation, Pope agreed to review whatever I wanted to send ahead of my arrival.

When I arrived in New York in January, Pope had received my package only a short time before, and was not prepared to make a decision about all the pieces. The bad news was that Boosey was too overloaded with large-scale choral works and songs to even consider *Singing Is So Good a Thing, The King's Contest,* or the song cycle I had sent. The good news was that they were still interested in the First Symphony. It wasn't until 1973, however—a year later—that Pope offered me a contract for the symphony, as well as for *English Girls* and *The Children of David.* All three were published in 1974. That same year, Boosey also accepted the Second Symphony, which was issued in 1988 as a pocket score. But in 1972, I still had no contract for the major works with Boosey or anyone else.

The rest of the U.S. trip cheered me up. In Chicago I renewed my friendship with William Ballard, who on January 23 conducted the premiere of *Singing Is So Good a Thing.* I had met Bill and Edith Ballard in Chicago in April 1966, when he conducted the Midwestern premiere of the chamber version of *The King's Contest* (then still known as *Zorobabel*) with his North Shore Congregation Israel chorus and members of the Chicago Symphony Orchestra. I had come down with the flu and had to remain in bed at the Ballard's house in Evanston for several days.

When I felt better, I wrote a round for each of their four children. They were about the ages of our four, and I had asked Edith about the interests and personalities of each. The eldest, Christopher, was reading *The Hobbit* at the time, so I picked from it the poem beginning "Sing all ye joyful" for an eight-part round. The eight children of our two families finally met about ten years later and sang it together (Doe stood in for Jennifer). Later, I turned the round into a concert piece with piano accompaniment for Robert Geary's Piedmont Choirs, and it has become the centerpiece of their International Children's Chorus Festival, the work that hundreds of children from many countries sing together. The success of this little round leads me to believe I should do more of my composing in bed.

From Chicago I flew to San Francisco for the Schola Cantorum premiere of *The Children of David,* under Royal Stanton, in Palo Alto. I then flew to Syracuse at the invitation of Donald B. Miller, who at the University of Southern California had written the first doctoral dissertation on my music. (There have now been eight, some of which describe my music in such complex terms I can hardly understand them.) I conducted madrigals and motets, and spoke to students and to the general public.

When I returned to London, I still did not feel like beginning a major work. For the first time in years, I had no commission, and this contributed to my low spirits. I nevertheless went on with the revision and orchestration of *The King's Contest*.

All the children did well in their London schools, but they were delighted to come back to America. They now say that they were glad to experience a year in another country. I'm not so sure. I regret putting the family through an unnecessary trial because of my own disappointments.

* * *

My interest in opera, acquired in Vienna, continued in London, and for the first time I seriously contemplated writing one. This may have been partly because I had given up on symphonies. There were so many glorious works for orchestra in the repertoire, including many from the twentieth century, that additions from relatively unknown composers were not needed—except for world premieres! I've never been interested in composing a work that will be produced only once.

But the situation in the opera world seemed different. There were pitifully few modern works in the repertoire, and not nearly so many great classic operas as there were great orchestral works. It seemed to me that the opera world badly *needed* good, new works. All my life I had set words to music, often in a dramatic context, so I was not afraid of the form.

My father's play, *John Brown*, had for years been in my mind as an ideal subject for opera. I remembered my enthusiasm for a possible *Tartuffe* opera, but if I were ever going to work with my father on *John Brown*, I had better do it soon, as he was already eighty-two. When I had finished the orchestration of *The King's Contest*, I wrote to my father and asked if he was still willing to help me turn his play into an opera libretto. When he replied that he was, I assumed that he would wait for my return to America and work on this jointly.

I went to several libraries in London and found biographies of Brown written decades later than my father's play. His view of Brown and of the national struggle over slavery were based chiefly on the 1910 biography by Oswald Garrison Villard. As I read the meticulously re-searched, objective biography published in 1970 by Stephen B. Oates, *To Purge This Land with Blood,* I saw that Brown was much more than a lone fanatic, and I knew that my opera would be quite different from my father's play. The play's blank-verse poetry was powerful, but as history—while accepted as reasonably accurate in 1938—the play would not pass muster forty years later. Although Brown had many African-American friends and associates, there was no black person of any consequence in the play, and the most sympathetic character was not Brown himself, but one of his comrades.

It has taken Americans many generations to understand the real story of John Brown, and most people still believe the myths and fabri-cations that have held sway for a century and a half. I will write about this controversial subject later, but for now will only relate the sad end to the possibility of working with my father.

A month or two after I had begun my research, I was astonished to receive in the mail my father's complete *John Brown* libretto. As I read it, my surprise turned to a most painful distress. Gone was the great poetry; in its place was the kind of terse dialogue he must have modeled on bad translations of Italian operas. He had underlined every word that was to be accented. I could see that even in the unlikely event that I could persuade him to accept my ideas for changes, he had lost his superb writing skill. He was diagnosed with Alzheimer's disease several years later (confirmed at death by an autopsy), and I realized that the disease had already damaged his brain when he wrote the libretto.

From London, I thanked him for what he had written, and wrote that I hoped together we could work out the changes I needed after I returned to California. (He and my mother had moved to Palo Alto in 1964.) His answer was that he didn't see why changes were needed—he thought I was going to compose an opera on his play, not alter it. I reminded him that as this would be my first opera, I wanted to plan it carefully, always with the *musical* form in mind. In fact, I had serious misgivings about such an extensive undertaking as my first step into the minefield of opera. Perhaps it would be better if I went back to *Tar-tuffe*. In any case, we could discuss *John Brown* when I came home.

That's how we left it until I saw him again. By then, however, we were both acutely concerned about the dementia that my mother was suffering. She died in 1974 of atherosclerosis. I did not wish to add to my father's grief by bringing up the subject of *John Brown*, and he never mentioned it again.

* * *

The summer before we returned to America, our family took an excursion to the town of Dorking in Surrey, where Ralph Vaughan Williams had lived for much of his life. I had read several books about the English composer, and had learned something important from him. His music was quintessentially English, reflective of the folk music and countryside of his surroundings. He cultivated his own garden, so to speak, conducting a chorus in Dorking close to his roots. He had studied with Ravel for three months as a young man, but Ravel later said that Vaughan Williams was his only student who hadn't ended up writing like Ravel. Vaughan Williams was proudly English, and I took the point to heart. Many of the works I wrote when I returned home—*John Brown, American Madrigals*, and many smaller pieces—are based on American themes.

But there's a downside to excluding all foreign subjects: witness the recent practice of American opera impresarios who became fixated on the here and now—"CNN operas," as one critic called them. These often missed the universality that marks so many of the great operas of the past. Verdi's best operas are on Shakespeare plays; only one of Puccini's great hits is set in Italy, and that one—*Tosca*—is based on a French play; Mozart and Rossini's *Figaro* operas are derived from the plays of a Frenchman. While there are, of course, examples of fine locally based operas, my point is simply that a composer should look *everywhere* for subjects worthy of opera—they are hard enough to find without limiting the time or place.

14

PROFESSOR NONTROPPO TO THE JAYHAWK

Back in San Francisco, I was soon busy with several choral commissions. It's hard to turn commissions down, as they are an important part of a composer's income, but I was eager for something new. Opera was stirring in the back of my mind. I began attending more performances in San Francisco, discovering what I liked and what I didn't. I had given up on *John Brown* for the time being, but had not settled on *Tartuffe* or anything else to take its place. I will mention briefly some of the more unusual works that occupied me from 1973 until 1977, when I bit the operatic bullet. You will note that in most of them, I had a hand in shaping the text.

"Professor Nontroppo's Music Dictionary" was commissioned for the 1973 European tour of the United States Honor Choir, Dr. Charlene Archibeque, conductor. My "libretto" consists entirely of Italian musical terms, which the chorus illustrates: *allegro con spirito, marcatissimo, sotto voce, furioso, subito piano, fermata lunga*—these are understood in every country. It's probably my funniest choral piece, and it has been particularly well received at choral conventions.

In February 1974, I received a commission to write a fifteen-minute work for baritone solo, large chorus, and orchestra for the convention of the Music Educators National Conference in Anaheim, California. I had one month to produce it. Luckily, I immediately found in my file a great poem I thought would perfectly fit the occasion—Archibald MacLeish's "Speech to a Crowd," addressed to those "perennial awaiters of messages" who expect some other power to solve humanity's problems. It is a strong and archetypal American poem, but I was wrong about it fitting the occasion. MacLeish's poem is considered sacrilege by some people, and so was my piece, which used several hymn tunes to point up the text. Here is how the thirty-six-line poem begins:

> Tell me, my patient friends, awaiters of messages,
> From what other shore, from what stranger,
> Whence, was the word to come? Who was to lesson you?
> Listeners under a child's crib in a manger,
> Listeners once by the oracles, now by the transoms,
> Whom are you waiting for? Who do you think will explain?

This is no more sacrilegious than is the old adage "God helps those who help themselves." But the premiere of *Speech to a Crowd* took place in Orange County, where creationists were still fighting Darwin.

There is abundant emotion and variety in the poem and (I think) in the music, but it is hardly ever performed. Several of my colleagues think *Speech to a Crowd*, op. 44, is my best work, but some of the negative feedback I received—not for my music, but for setting such a text—makes me wonder: Am I really the only agnostic in the whole world of choral music? As I have explained earlier, I am neither religious nor antireligious, and it is hard to believe that any educated person would find either this poem or my music offensive.

Once again I had forgotten that large, choral-orchestral works were expected to be both old and religious, and unless they were by Bach, Handel, Mendelssohn, or Brahms, they should be in Latin. Choral audiences will occasionally put up with challenging ideas in English if the music is short and brazenly simple, but somehow a belief has taken root that massed singers with orchestra must sing only words that are liturgical or uplifting. This may be because choral music was for centuries the handmaiden of religion.

* * *

Who is in the audience at a choral concert? The answer to that question sometimes dictates the program and its reception. Most choral directors will tell you that the size of the average choral audience is directly proportional to the number of singers on stage. That's because most of the listeners are family or friends of the singers. It is not the same audience that goes to the symphony, the opera, or (especially) to hear chamber music.

But here's an exception. Because it was a concert underwritten by the San Francisco Arts Commission, it was able to defy most of the maxims I have just noted. On June 16, 1974, I was given a chance to conduct the new version of *The King's Contest* with a large chorus and full orchestra (San Francisco Symphony players) in the Opera House. Each of the three works on the program was composed in the twentieth century; all were secular and none were in Latin. Furthermore, there was an audience of a couple of thousand. Not only were the singers and orchestra paid for, but the concert was free to the public. Not your average underfunded choral concert.

The dramatic cantata I had orchestrated in London was performed between a work by Maurice Ohana, in Spanish, and Prokofiev's *Alexander Nevsky,* in Russian. Winifred Baker's Civic Chorale sang all three works. The reader already knows that my text was neither provocative nor severe, but a delightful story about wine, women, and a king. The critics and audience responded to it more than to the other pieces—it was the only one in their own language—but don't expect to hear it at a choral concert anytime soon, except possibly in its original chamber version. In these days of government cutbacks at all levels, it is even more rare than it was then for a municipal-arts commission to pay for any concert, let alone such an expensive one.

* * *

After all the choral works, I was happy to receive a commission for a purely orchestral piece, especially from my hometown orchestra, the Topeka Symphony. I wrote an overture called *The Jayhawk*, a mythical bird that has come to be identified with Kansas and Kansans. It is an irreverent but sentimental bird with magic powers of transformation and disguise. The overture begins with a mysterious description of the birth of the jayhawk in the rock-chalk hills of Kansas (fluttering wings in the woodwinds) and eases into the famous college cheer that KU students perform when their football or basketball teams are in dire peril. My father had written a popular booklet on the subject, and I knew it would give opportunities for humor and variety, as most of the jayhawk's legendary adventures were practical jokes. He might be called an ornithological Till Eulenspiegel. *The Jayhawk: Magic Bird Overture,* op. 43, has become my most popular orchestral work.

Through my own poor planning, I had to write *The Jayhawk* so quickly that I borrowed some tunes—"Impertinence" and "The Happy

Drunken Organ Grinder"—from my piano pieces, *Whims* (the titles themselves are rather jayhawkish). Friends let me use their house in the hills of Inverness for three days, during which I was able to sketch out the complete overture. In a month the orchestration was done. I copied the parts myself and sent them to Topeka in time for the first rehearsal. The premiere took place March 19, 1975, under Dr. Everett Fetter. Doe and I brought my eighty-five-year-old father with us, and each member of the audience received a copy of his Jayhawk booklet. He was delighted to take a bow, to give an interview, and to see those few old friends who remained. One of them was the noted psychiatrist and author Karl Menninger, who had attended elementary school with Dad and later played chess with him.

A bicentennial choral commission came later that year from the well-known composer/conductor Lloyd Pfautsch and his Dallas Civic Chorus. For a long time I had wanted to write a group of madrigals based on American folk songs—real madrigals, not simply settings or arrangements—and this was an ideal opportunity.

In my note to the published score I wrote, "While the classic English and Italian madrigals were written for social singing by individuals, part singing in America—particularly in this century—has been done chiefly by choral groups with a view toward public performance. These *American Madrigals* [op. 46] are therefore intended for mixed chorus; they may be sung *a cappella*, with piano, or with instrumental ensemble. [The San Francisco Girls Chorus later commissioned a version for treble voices.] The folk material, both words and music, has been altered, added to and juxtaposed at will in an attempt to provide polyphonic, madrigal-like pieces with a specifically American flavor."

The five folk songs I chose were "Kind Miss," "He's Gone Away," "Kansas Boys," "Adam's Bride (A Marriage Lesson)," and "New York Girls." Each piece in both versions has been published separately, and they have been sung by U.S. choruses on tour in many countries as representative of American music—also by the BBC Singers and other European and Asian choruses. Thank you, Vaughan Williams, for teaching me to cultivate my own garden.

The text for the beautiful old folk song used in "Adam's Bride" had its origin in lines written in the fifteenth century by the revered German monk and writer Thomas à Kempis, the putative author of the famous *Imitation of Christ*. Some of the lines require historical perspective for women today. The folk text sounds quaint at best, and sexist if taken out of context. But it is nothing more than a medieval retelling of the biblical story about the first couple to be joined together.

> This woman was not taken from Adam's head, we know;
> And she must not rule over him, 'tis evidently so. . . .
> This woman she was taken from under Adam's arm;
> And she must be protected from injury and harm.
> This woman she was taken from near to Adam's heart,
> By which we are directed that they should never part.

Considered in this context, the poem is tender and touching, but for some modern young women, I can understand why it is difficult to accept. I urge them to consider context as simply an awareness of history. Are we to ban all stories from the past that include ideas we no longer accept? That would include hundreds of biblical and folk stories that we are accustomed to understand metaphorically.

✿ ✿ ✿

After so many short pieces for chorus and instruments, I was longing to tackle something I would have to grow into. Around the beginning of 1977 I decided to take the plunge: it was time to find out whether I could write a successful opera. My thoughts went back to the exhilarating ACT production of *Tartuffe*. I looked up the notes I had made, read the play again, and couldn't wait to get started.

15

OPERA 101

Composing *Tartuffe*

Ninety-nine out of a hundred first operas die at birth. Musical form is like a machine—the more moving parts there are, the more they are liable to malfunction. No musical form has more ways to fail than opera. Wagner called it the *Gesamtkunstwerk*—the "complete work of art." It combines singing, acting, dancing, orchestral music, drama, poetry, and scenic art—all thrown together to fill an entire evening. Failure of one element can result in a *gesamt* failure.

Many operas are doomed before a note has been written. Schubert comes to mind. The greatest songwriter in history—and many of his songs were *dramatic*—composed ten operas, none of which has passed the test of time. He didn't seem to care what happened on stage. He wrote so fluently that he would set to music any half-baked libretto a friend handed him. Unlike the rest of us, he was an inexhaustible fountain of melody. As H. L. Mencken once wrote, "The fellow was scarcely human. His merest belch was as lovely as the song of the sirens."

We mortals have to be more careful with our belches. I was old enough (fifty-two) to know how risky a first opera is, and was determined to do everything I could to improve my chances. I believed absolutely in Molière's play. *Tartuffe* was a perfect vehicle for comic opera, but an opera is not a play set to music. (I can't believe how many people think it is.) It's a mixture of musical and dramatic forms. I felt sure that with such a great play to start with, I could write my own libretto. Librettos don't require great poetry so much as they do effective words that sing well—words that come naturally, not literary words, but those that we speak every day. And I had always been a ham anyway—I acted in school plays, told stories, mimicked voices, and regularly attended plays and movies.

My study began with my three favorite comic operas—*The Marriage of Figaro, The Barber of Seville,* and *Falstaff*. All were made from plays, so I compared the original of each with its opera libretto, asking myself why the librettist and composer made the changes they did. I say librettist *and* composer because Mozart, Rossini, and Verdi were the dramatists as much or more than were the librettists Da Ponte, Sterbini, and Boito. All three composers had written many operas and were accustomed to calling the shots. Composers often hired librettists simply to put the composers' scenarios into verse. With Verdi, Rossini, or Puccini, if the libretto wasn't done to his satisfaction, he would make the poet do it over again or hire someone else.

What differentiates the opera composer from other composers is a theatrical sense. A good academic poet and a fine string-quartet composer will probably not make a good opera team. The best thing about being both librettist and composer is that when the two get into a fight, the composer always wins. (Except for Wagner; according to my friend Larry Hancock, when Wagner got into a fight with his librettist [himself], the librettist always won.) Maybe that's why Wagner wrote five-hour operas. The composer is the one who *should* win that battle. If a good melody doesn't quite fit the words, I don't have to change the melody; I can alter the words or tweak words *and* melody. And the composer doesn't have to worry about bruising the ego of the librettist. Every page of every libretto I have written has been changed by the composer—me—as he wrote the music. Try doing that with the work of a real poet, and then find yourself a good witness-protection program.

I am not the only composer today who writes his own librettos. And I am not so foolish as to claim that librettos written by composers make better operas than those composed in collaboration with a librettist. The opposite appears to be more true. The most popular operas in history—except those by Wagner—were collaborations. I'm sure one could make a long, convincing list of the *dangers* that face us composers who write our own librettos. Nevertheless, we do have some important advantages.

To begin with, we can plan the opera's scenes ahead of time. Poetic form is not the same as musical form. As a choral composer I had learned not to slavishly adhere to a poem's outer shape, but to follow its dramatic or psychological form. (See appendix 1 for my article "The Text Trap," a discussion of the relationship between poetic and musical form.)

In planning an opera, a librettist should continually consult the composer on the placement and timing of arias, recitatives, duets, and ensembles. Even composers who don't want any of those "old-fashioned" forms must still make sure that the music will have opportunities for variety, unity, and drama, and these are best devised in the libretto stage. So I should add to the list of a composer/librettist's advantages the *most* important—the opportunity to choose the subject. I would never have chosen some of the stories I have seen turned into operas: *The Great Gatsby, Moby Dick,* and *An American Tragedy,* to name just three. They simply did not seem to me to offer enough variety of characters and action; but of course, we all have different ideas about what makes a good opera. *Vive la différence!*

I learned much from comparing plays with librettos, but more from conducting, singing, and seeing operas live on stage. It's often remarked by comedians that "timing is everything." In the spoken theater, the actor or director determines the timing, but in opera it's usually the composer. The music tells the singer exactly when to begin singing, how quickly to move downstage, how slowly to deliver a line, when and how long to pause—even which words to accent. This is why I say that opera composers must have a theatrical sense. There's still plenty for operatic stage directors to do—even more than in the spoken theater, where they don't have to move choruses around, coordinate actions with music, or correct the composer's miscalculations.

When I began to plan how I was going to turn *Tartuffe* into an opera, two obstacles appeared immediately. The play was too long, and was dominated by men. Opera needs more vocal variety than theater does. I saw that this was a chance to kill two birds with one stone: cut out the male character Cléante, who may not have been in Molière's banned first version anyway. Cléante pretends to be the voice of reason, speaking platitudes to placate the censors, tediously repeating that it is not *true* religion that is being mocked, but only false piety for selfish ends. I simply removed his part and gave the voice-of-reason role to his sister,

Elmire, enlarging her part in the process. The maid, Dorine, gets an aria in the first act to strengthen her characterization; she also gets a lot of coloratura laughter.

The play is in five acts, the opera in three. I arranged the action so that each of the acts ends with an ensemble. It's a truism that tragedy is lonely, comedy gregarious: "Laugh and the world laughs with you; cry and you cry alone." So it's natural for comic operas to conclude their acts with hubbubs or celebrations. Molière's *deus-ex-machina* ending has been universally criticized; he was no doubt forced to add it to get past the censors. In my version, the bailiff, police officer, and envoy from the king are Damis, Valère, and Mariane in disguise. A cardinal rule of drama is that the protagonists must solve their own problems, and disguise is a hallowed tradition of *commedia dell' arte*, which was the source of both comic opera and Molière's plays. Disguise worked out so naturally in my finale that I had a weird feeling that it was what Molière himself had in mind! Why else would the "bailiff" tell Orgon, "Your family's long been dear to me"? This gives Damis's words added resonance and lets the audience see that although he is helping his father, he is still angry with him. I divided into two parts the officer's role in Molière's finale, giving part of it to an "envoy" (Mariane), so that she could join the fun. This gives the ending an extra twist by allowing the young people to outwit the older.

I mentioned earlier that the inspiring ACT production I saw used the virtuoso translation by Richard Wilbur. Many people have asked why I didn't use that version for my opera. For one thing, I'm quite sure Mr. Wilbur would never have given me permission to chop up his translation. Furthermore, he follows Molière's alexandrine poetic meter exactly: rhymed couplets with twelve syllables per line. Such a formal structure is hard enough to bring off in a long play; in an opera it would hobble the music. I used the kind of verse found in *La Boheme*, that is, different forms for different musical characterizations. For example, Madame Pernelle is a rigid, authoritarian kind of person, so I gave her formal, rigid verse patterns:

> Good morals here
> Are sorely missed;
> Good manners simply
> Don't exist.

Her son, Orgon, bewitched by Tartuffe's phony piety, sings the clichés
of operatic sanctimony. For that, I gave him expansive, mawkish lines,
so different in form from those of his mother:

> Every day at church Tartuffe was there,
> Kneeling just across from me in pious prayer.
> The fervor of his feeling soon caught every eye;
> He'd kiss the earth, and wail, and weep, and sigh.

I've often been asked how long it took to write the opera. I don't know
why it matters, but the answer is three years:

- Study and writing the libretto, three months
- Writing the music (first draft), one year and three months
- Editing and copying the piano-vocal score, three months
- Orchestration, nine months
- Copying and checking orchestral parts, six months

Note on orchestration: After ten or twenty pages of a draft that I wrote
in pencil, I found I could work directly in ink, saving the time it would
take to make a final ink copy. I often listened to the San Francisco
Giants' baseball games on the radio at the same time. Orchestration is
done in the head. Once the decisions have been made, writing it down
becomes a simple, but exacting, manual task, requiring care but little
thought. (And the Giants weren't so thrilling then as they were later.)

There were interruptions for several commissioned choral pieces
and for family matters. (Bringing up four children in San Francisco in
the 1970s was no picnic.) But on December 5, 1979, I wrote "End of
opera" at the bottom of page 1,092 of the orchestral score.

I kept a journal that year and during parts of 1980 and 1981. These
years cover the frustrating months of trying to get the San Francisco
Opera to premiere *Tartuffe,* then the rehearsal period, the first performances, and the aftermath. My journals will give a more immediate and
personal view of this roller-coaster ride than anything I could describe
now, so I will reproduce excerpts.

16

OPERA 102
The Real Opera World

When I wrote *Tartuffe*, I had in mind the seventeen hundred-seat Curran Theater in downtown San Francisco. This was the home of Spring Opera Theater, an arm of the San Francisco Opera. Its season, more adventurous and theatrical than the fall season at the Opera House, consisted of four operas every spring.

But because *Tartuffe*'s premiere took place in the smaller Herbst Theater, and because many smaller companies and universities have performed the opera with its *reduced* orchestration, it is often mistakenly considered a chamber opera. That misconception has dogged this opera from the beginning, and I hope you will forgive me for mentioning it again. Its original orchestra is about the size of Stravinsky's in *The Rake's Progress* and slightly larger than Mozart's in his three Da Ponte operas, all of which are regularly performed in large halls.

The first step in getting the San Francisco Opera to premiere *Tartuffe* was to play and sing the score several times for various assistant conductors and stage directors. From May 1979 until February 1980, I was given the royal runaround. There was hope; then there was not. It was a nerve-racking process.

* * *

Journal, December 14, 1979: My fatigue and discouragement have lately been taking me on an escapist path. . . . Maybe the time has come to stop. There is a world to enjoy—books to read, things to know, places to see, people to meet, and music to enjoy as a human being. . . . I long to rest, and I also see much that needs doing in the world that has nothing to do with music. But mostly I am tired of pushing against indifference.

* * *

Journal, February 25, 1980: David Agler phoned last Thursday. [Agler was the resident conductor at SF Opera.] He began by apologizing for not calling sooner. That seemed slightly ominous. People don't apologize or beat around the bush if they have *good* news. He described how he had put Mr. Adler [general director of the company] on a flight to Europe, handing him the *Tartuffe* score with the words, "This is what we want to do for the American Opera Project this spring. Please look it over on the flight, and as soon as you land, send me a Telex: 'Yes' or 'No.'" But why am *I* beating around the bush? David said he had just received a Telex from Adler—the word was "Yes"— and "it is our intention, if you are still willing, to produce *Tartuffe* for the American Opera Project." Was I willing? Was Martin Luther a Lutheran? The performances would be in Herbst Theater, next door to the Opera House, May 27 and 28, 1980. [By this time, Spring Opera was on its last legs, and everyone I knew at the Opera House told me that this new NEA-funded American Opera Project would be the best place for *Tartuffe*'s premiere.]

* * *

The rehearsal period was both a joy and a trial for me. The opera had the great good fortune of a cast that was magnificent; many of these singers went on to stellar careers at the Met and other important houses. John Del Carlo, our Tartuffe, became one of the principal buffo basses in the world; Tom Hammons (Orgon) is still at the Met; Susan Quittmeyer (Elmire) was in demand at the Met and elsewhere until she gave up singing to raise a family; Evelyn de la Rosa stole the first act with her acting and musically brilliant Dorine (she has sung for many U.S. opera companies); Rebecca Cook (Mariane), Edward Huls (Damis), Leslie Richards (Madame Pernelle), and Robert Tate (Valere) were all excellent. Steven Eldredge was the splendid principal pianist. David Agler was a brilliant and sensitive conductor, and Nancy Rhodes's staging was superb. How many rookie opera composers have that kind of luck?

The downside of the rehearsal period was the ambiguity of my presence. The NEA grant specified that the composer was to be on hand throughout the rehearsal process, and I was paid accordingly. But as many composers who have lived through an opera premiere know, their work is sometimes considered ended when they hand over the score to the company. I was asked not to offer suggestions during rehearsals. That's not surprising; singers can't be expected to take directions from both director and composer. Opera people are used to performing the works of dead composers; live ones are sometimes in the way. As this was my first opera, it took a while for me to know how to act, to curb my impulsiveness.

I was overconfident, and this came across sometimes as conceited. I was absolutely sure, once I heard this cast sing it, that my opera was going to be a big hit. But it seemed I was the only one who thought so. The singers and staff did not have the leisure to project a great success; they were too busy working. It was they who had to put the opera over. Many of them had previously been involved in premieres that had flopped. So it may have appeared to them that I was so in love with my own work that it clouded my judgment. After all, as the producer, Christine Bullin, told me later, *every* composer thinks his new work will be a hit. (Being right is evidently no excuse.)

When I balked at making cuts in the show, it played right into the egotistical-composer stereotype. However, I did accept three of the five suggested cuts, and later recommended that these cuts appear in the published score. Since then, I have suggested many other small cuts. Although I did everything I could to express my gratitude to all involved, then and later, I know that a more unassuming attitude and some humility would have made more friends.

The success of *Tartuffe* was immense; it was a turning point in my career. Kurt Herbert Adler became a firm supporter of my music, and nominated *Tartuffe* to be included in Opera America's first Showcase for New Works at its annual convention. He told the assembled leaders of the opera world that *Tartuffe* was such a success that for the final performance he had to call in the fire marshal to pacify a crowd trying to get into the hall after it was full. The reviews were almost unanimously enthusiastic.

But there was an important dissenter—a critic whose press pass Adler had earlier revoked because of her "insulting, caustic rudeness."

From that moment on, Stephanie von Buchau's reviews of the San Francisco Opera were pure poison. In the months before *Tartuffe*'s premiere, she had excoriated every one of the Spring Opera productions. For *Tartuffe*, her bile would not have mattered if the effect had been only local, but she wrote reviews in *Opera News* and the English magazine *Opera*; they were the only evaluations that the greater opera world saw. "*Tartuffe* was a bewilderingly eclectic affair," she wrote in one review, charging that I "imitated or directly quoted" a long list of composers while neglecting to mention that the audience was laughing with delight at the parodies and caricature. The overwhelming number of rave reviews of the premiere and of subsequent productions—and the opera's National Public Radio broadcasts—have undone some of the damage, but there's no telling how many large regional companies Ms. Buchau scared off. Fortunately, that kind of critic is rare.

Howard Scott, president of the publishing house G. Schirmer, came from New York to the dress rehearsals and performances of *Tartuffe*. He and his wife, a former singer, were enthusiastic. He asked me to publish with Schirmer exclusively (to which I agreed), wrote a check to cover my copying expenses, and later nominated *Tartuffe* for the Pulitzer Prize. (In vain, of course; judges for the Pulitzer still came chiefly from the avant-garde citadels of academia. No prize was given that year for music.) So intent was Scott on locking up my opera for Schirmer that he insisted I give him all the orchestral parts to take back to New York. I eventually talked him into returning them to me so that I could edit them. Making changes and cuts in the scores and parts took up most of the summer. But first, Doe and I drove down to La Jolla for a two-week vacation at the beach.

I missed my *Tartuffe* characters! After living with them for over three years, I had trouble letting them go.

* * *

In early January 1981, after a gap of almost nine months, I wrote in my journal again. I had been too busy and emotional to keep it going during the rehearsals, performances, and the aftermath; but later I wrote:

> I can now understand why the personal lives of so many actors are unstable. The real world isn't as real to them as their stage lives are. I had some personal problems all through the latter part of the previous year that I'm sure stemmed from a sense of unreality, from a

distressing letdown after the culmination of so much work and emotion, and from the boredom of having to spend all summer patching
up the scores and parts.

* * *

Journal, January 2, 1981: I was delighted to see Schirmer's confidence in *Tartuffe's* future. Howard Scott asked me to write an overture to the opera; when I told him that the first scene is virtually an
overture (a real overture would steal its thunder), he asked me to put
together an orchestral suite. [I have been asked the same thing by a
couple of orchestra conductors.] . . . I am frankly doubtful as to the
musical viability of a suite. The music is so intricately bound up with
situation, character, and satire, it might puzzle a symphony audience.
[Someday, if the opera makes its way into the larger and more important houses, a suite might make sense.]

* * *

Journal, January 4, 1981: I spent a lot of time studying and attending
operas during the fall season. Only Janacek's *Jenufa* made a deep
impression on me, though I enjoyed *Samson and Delilah* and *Don
Pasquale* very much. *Simon Boccanegra* was not nearly as good as
was its production a few years ago. I tried *Frau ohne Schatten* again
and was impressed mostly by its pretentiousness. *Arabella* was enjoy-
able in part, but hardly memorable. This year's production of *The
Magic Flute* was dreadfully slow and dull, as was Adler's conducting
of *Tristan*.

* * *

From this report you could conclude that I am no opera buff at all,
and in one sense of that term, you would be correct. I am not satisfied
to spend an entire evening and a lot of money to hear one or two good
singers, unless both the opera and the production are good enough to
keep me interested. I am easily bored. For a composer, perhaps that is
an asset; for an opera-goer, or any other kind of normal human being, it
can be a problem. Still, few things in this world are as thrilling and as
beautiful as a great production of a great opera.

By "great," I don't mean just the big, famous companies. While it is
true that only they can afford the top singers and directors, I have

sometimes been disappointed by their productions for various reasons. Their celebrity stars are hired as much as five years in advance; the voice we hear on stage is not the same voice it was five years before. And sometimes productions in big-budget houses overwhelm the opera and its singers in an attempt to be novel or to show off a director's "concept."

As an example of a smaller company where those defects hardly ever show up, I can recommend Opera San Jose. It is unique in this country: a resident ensemble (on the old German model) of gifted young singers who are given multi-year contracts. They perform not the smaller roles usually offered to young singers by major companies, but the principal roles—if the singers are ready for them. The company was founded in 1984 by an internationally acclaimed mezzo, the late Irene Dalis, a native of San Jose, who carefully nurtured the company and its singers for thirty years. I have enjoyed many thrilling performances by these excellent young voices in productions that maintain high dramatic and musical standards. There are many other regional companies, of course, that also offer first-rate productions, so don't think for a minute that only celebrities are worth hearing.

17

THE LIFE AND DEATH OF JOHN BROWN

John Brown was finally taking shape in my mind. Throughout the fall and winter I read more than a dozen books about the man and the period. I began making notes and trying to decide which scenes would be indispensable.

John Brown was going to have much in common with Mussorgsky's *Boris Godunov:* a controversial protagonist, a national catastrophe, and a large and important part for the chorus—but not the expensive sets and costumes! The story is nothing less than why the Civil War was fought. Brown's Old Testament message was simple: you cannot have both injustice and peace. This proved to be an accurate prophecy; it took a national cataclysm to end slavery. Even the love story between Brown's son and a girl from a pacifist family points up a poignant human side of the story, a contrast to the momentous events around John Brown, Frederick Douglass, Jeb Stuart, and partisans from the North and the South.

I became immersed in this history. I have already mentioned that my father hated injustice; he passed that emotion on to his children, and it is evident in his *John Brown* play. Not only as a Kansan did I feel close to the John Brown story, but also because my grandfather, Hiram Wheeler Lewis, fought with the Union Army in the Civil War. His own father must have known John Brown; they both worked in animal husbandry in a small corner of northeast Ohio.

After almost a year of research, I made a rough scenario and took it to Amherst, Massachusetts, where I visited Professor Stephen B. Oates, at that time the foremost biographer of John Brown. After a memorable three-hour discussion, he said I was on the right track and agreed to read the libretto as it developed. After I held readings of preliminary drafts, I sent the libretto to Oates, scene by scene, so that he could correct any unacceptable compromises I had made with historical fact. Historical dramas must always telescope events, times, and places; they tell minor lies to show major truths.

[See appendix B—my afterword to the libretto. Though it is too extensive for the body of this book, I include it because the fascinating history of this period is crucial to my opera. The afterword is an examination of the controversies around John Brown and the difficulties of turning his story into an opera.]

❀ ❀ ❀

Finally I began the music. The first notes I composed were an original melody for Brown's favorite hymn, "Blow Ye the Trumpet." Why didn't I use the existing tune? Because research in several libraries of old hymnals did not turn up any melody that matched the words for the hymn quoted at the end of Oates's biography.

[See appendix C for my article "The Hymn Bandit," published in *Voice*, the magazine of Chorus America. It tells how an author's mistake became a composer's inspiration.]

❀ ❀ ❀

I finished the full score of Act I in the early 1980s. During those years I also had to make a reduced orchestral score for *Tartuffe* and to write various choral pieces on commission to help pay for the copying. Meanwhile, two of the choruses from *John Brown* were published: "Dan-u-el" and "Blow Ye the Trumpet"; both became best sellers. Several years later I completed the full score for all three acts and began to make a piano reduction. That was the most painful part of the process. To reduce a complex orchestral work to a piano score is like trying to shrink a multicolored, wall-sized mural onto a black-and-white postcard—only a lot harder.

While waiting for the opera to be produced, I extracted from it a five-movement suite, *Songs of the Slave*. This was commissioned by a consortium of choral and orchestral groups in the Los Angeles area, directed by Dr. James E. Smith. It was a godsend. It gave me a paid opportunity to try out parts of the opera and to use the recording to interest opera companies in *John Brown*. I already had a demo tape with my young friends Deborah Voigt, Mark Delavan, and David Oker-lund singing some of the arias with piano accompaniment. Schirmer published the suite, which has had nearly a hundred performances. Its warm reception encouraged me not to give up on the opera.

I was particularly happy to hear the suite performed in Washington, DC, as the featured work of the 1995 convention of the American Choral Directors Association, expertly conducted by my old friend Dr. William Hall. The Washington Opera Orchestra accompanied three choral groups: two black (the chorales of Moses Hogan and Brazeal Dennard) and one white (the William Hall Chorale). At my request, the singers were mixed together. One performance was in the Kennedy Center, but the other was more emotional for me. It was performed in Constitution Hall, where in 1939, the great singer Marian Anderson had been refused permission to sing because she was black. I had been in the Stanford Chorus when we sang the Brahms Alto Rhapsody with her and the San Francisco Symphony under William Steinberg.

I recognized that at three hours and a quarter, *John Brown* was much too long, but I thought it would be wise to get some input about cuts from the yet-to-be-found commissioning company. After all, I would be asking for the commission of an already-completed opera. That's not the way it's usually done, but I have seen too many operas fail because the composer was trying to carry out other people's ideas. I have turned down opera commissions when the already-chosen subject matter did not appeal to me. After the premiere of *Tartuffe*, Tito Ca-pobianco offered me a commission to write a one-act piece for San Diego Opera based on O. Henry's short story, "The Gift of the Magi." On paper it is a touching little tale, but for opera, the young lovers are too bland, too undifferentiated, and the plot amounts to little more than a setup for the trick ending. (I must admit, however, that my friend David Conte found a way around some of these problems, and has written an often-performed one-act opera on O. Henry's story.) When I take on such a formidable project as opera, I want to pick the subject and work it out in my own way at my own time. Stravinsky had no problem getting commissions for works he had already composed, but for the likes of me, that strategy has been financially precarious.

After the Washington DC performances of the suite from *John Brown* came the long, frustrating years of waiting for a company to premiere the full opera. It had a "workshop" that didn't work, and the opera was rejected by companies afraid of the controversy around John Brown. The director of one major company liked the opera and had already tentatively cast some of the roles, but in the end he called me to say that he could not fund it because his conservative board told him that "John Brown was not a very nice man"—as if Boris Godunov, Macbeth, Don Giovanni, Eugene Onegin, Peter Grimes, and many other operatic subjects were "nice" men!

18

EVERYONE SANG

I had to put *John Brown* away for several years and work on other vocal projects: *To an Absent Love*—a group of songs for soprano; several choral cycles—*American Trio, Choral Variations on American Folk Songs, Earth My Song, Missa Brevis ("Trinity"), Three Motets, Winging Wildly, Suite for Chorus,* and *Peace Motets*—as well as a number of shorter choral pieces. Some of these choral works are discussed in appendix A.

I have already mentioned the many catches, canons, and other occasional pieces I have written for friends and family. Sometimes these became published concert works, such as "A Wedding Gift," written for my pianist friend, William Corbett-Jones, and his charming young bride, Louise DiMattio. The wedding took place in our living room on December 22, 1979; the guests sang the SATB choral parts, Camilla Wicks played violin, and yours truly was at the piano.

Bill and Louise have been among our closest friends for decades, sharing our interest in books, walks, movies, and of course, music. Bill has a near-photographic memory; if I didn't have time to read a book Bill had read, I could simply go for a walk with him, ask a few questions about the book, and receive as much of it verbatim as I wished to know.

Another of our closest friends, Roy Bogas, is also a celebrated pianist. He, too, married a charming young woman, Susan Brubaker (what is it about pianists that attracts beautiful blondes?). Susan later organized a surprise party for Roy's fiftieth birthday, for which I composed a musical joke—a surprise piece tailored for the voices and instruments of the invited guests, most of them performers. As Roy (like Bill) is an incorrigible fan of puns and limericks, his gift was incorrigible:

> That prodigal pianist named Bogas
> Stayed young without Jung, yeast or yogas;
> At fifty his trilling
> Was nifty and thrilling;
> His octaves were sheer hocus pogas.

❊ ❊ ❊

Two works from this between-operas period had their origin in the Beyond War movement that Donata was active in. "Las Americas Unidas," in Spanish and English, was commissioned for the Spacebridge of the Americas, December 14, 1986, the first time live television linked five continents by satellite. I conducted members of the San Francisco Chamber Singers, The Golden Gate Boys Choir, soprano Kathy Burch, and an instrumental ensemble.

The other Beyond War–inspired piece, "Island in Space," is one of my strongest *a cappella* works for mixed chorus. It was commissioned for a 1990 tour to the Soviet Union and Poland by the California State University (Chico) Choir, Dr. Sharon Paul, conductor. I adapted the principal text from a speech by Russell Schweikart, the Apollo 9 astronaut who was the first person to make an unattached walk in space. The text describes his emotions when he saw the earth at that distance: "You can't imagine how many borders and boundaries you cross, and you don't even see them. The earth is a whole—so beautiful, so small, and so fragile. You realize that on that small spot is everything that means anything to you: all history, all poetry, all music, all art, death, birth, love, tears, all games, all joy—all on that small spot."

I added to Schweikart's words two other texts: *Dona nobis pacem* (grant us peace), and a fragment from a poem by Archibald MacLeish. Doctor Paul told me that when the choir sang the work in the Warsaw Cathedral, there was not a dry eye in either the chorus or the audience. These words have the same effect on me.

Winging Wildly, for mixed chorus, is also based on highly emotional texts; I consider it my best choral cycle. It was jointly commissioned in 1996 by Robert Geary's San Francisco Chamber Singers (now called Volti), Seán Deibler's Music Group of Philadelphia, and Robert Trocchia's Lancaster (OH) Chorale, all of whom first performed it in the spring of 1998. It is a work in three movements, with both poetic and musical unity. Each poem uses birds as a metaphor for various aspects of human life, and all of them refer to singing. The poems are Sara Teasdale's "Dusk in June" (called "Birds at Dusk" in my cycle); Paul Laurence Dunbar's "The Caged Bird" (his original title was "Sympathy"); and Siegfried Sassoon's "Everyone Sang." The second piece, "The Caged Bird," is better known by the final line of Dunbar's poem, "I know why the caged bird sings," which the late poet Maya Angelou used as the title of her celebrated autobiography.

In my earlier discussion of *Singing Is So Good a Thing*, I mentioned that the Elgin Choral Society, which had commissioned the work for its twenty-fifth anniversary, later commissioned me to compose a substantial piece for its fiftieth anniversary. I put together three poems by my father to form a cycle of life, death, and rebirth: *Earth My Song*, op. 61. The first is one of my favorite poems, and I used it again—with completely different music—in a song cycle for baritone and orchestra, *From The Heartland*, op. 77, commissioned in 2009 by Kent Nagano and the Berkeley Symphony Orchestra.

I Could Hear the Least Bird Sing

In my boyhood, in the spring,
When the world and I were young,
I could hear the least bird sing
Songs no bird has ever sung.

And in summer, in my youth,
As an eagle climbs the sun,
I could reach the starry truth
Men of earth have never won.

Now in autumn, in the fall,
When the birds are flying far,
All the truth seems very small
And a star is but a star.

But in winter, in old age,
I shall go where truth is found:
Earth my song and earth my wage,
In the still and starless ground.

In *Earth My Song*, this desolate ending is followed by a poem even more desolate, "Isle of the Dead." Because the poem is so powerful, and because its title has such a resonant history, I added a special note for choruses and audiences:

> In 1880, the Swiss artist Arnold Böcklin painted *The Isle of the Dead*, showing a forbidding cliff surrounded by dark water. It became one of the most famous paintings of its time, and continued its hold on artists for generations—writers, poets, painters, even musicians. Rachmaninoff composed a ghostly tone-poem on the subject in 1909. My father's poem, "Isle of the Dead," was inspired by this painting, and also perhaps by Rachmaninoff's composition. But the poem is not about death itself, I think; rather, it uses death as a metaphor for the deep depression that sometimes comes upon our souls, usually at night, and kills our most precious gift—the ability to love. The poem is a nightmare of alienation, estrangement from those who are dearest to us—a living death. I know that my father experienced such darkness at times, as did Rachmaninoff. I wish I had asked my father about "Isle of the Dead" while he was alive. It has always fascinated me, but frightened me too. Perhaps this explains why I did not ask him, and why it took me so long to feel that I understood the poem well enough to compose music for it. Other interpretations are possible, of course, but this is the one that feels right to me, and brought forth the most disconsolate music I have ever written.

Isle of the Dead

Beyond the fog of the tide
In the night,
When the moon fades,
The graves open.
First the old men
Clamber about the shore,
Staring seaward,
Searching among the sods.
Behind them the old women,
Blinking, walk the pale grass,
Shuffling among the sods.
Then the men in their prime
And the women in their beauty,
Separately, searching.

And last the children,
Boys and girls together,
Whimpering in the unaccustomed light,
Crawl among the sods.
Neither the old men
See their old women,
Nor the men in their prime
Their women in their beauty,
Nor any their children.
Nor do the children
Discover father or mother.
For this is the first intimation
And outpost of hell,
Found by the living
Among loved ones
In the depths of the night.

The third piece, "Rebirth" (original title: "End of Summer"), returns in its final pages to the music that began the cycle. *Earth My Song* was premiered in Elgin, Illinois, May 31, 1997, under the direction of John G. Slawson.

❀ ❀ ❀

Closer to home, I have been part of the Forest Hill Musical Days festivals held in San Francisco most summers since 2003. These have been sponsored and organized by conductor Kent Nagano and his wife, the pianist Mari Kodama, residents for many years in the Forest Hill district. Through the efforts and connections of these celebrated international musicians, I have been privileged to work with some of the finest European, Asian, and American performers. As composer-in-residence, my songs and chamber music have been regular parts of these programs, for which I am greatly indebted not only to the Naganos but also to the enthusiastic and tireless work of the FHMD board.

❀ ❀ ❀

During the long period between the composition of *John Brown* and its premiere, I also wrote another opera: *The Rivals*, based on the Restoration comedy by Richard Sheridan. More about that after the end of the *John Brown* adventure.

19

JOHN BROWN'S RESURRECTION

After its long hibernation, I took the dusty score off the shelf and found that I could look at *John Brown* with a more objective eye. I was able to revise the opera, cutting forty-five minutes quite painlessly. Merging these revisions into the printed scores and parts would be an enormous job not only for me, but also for my excellent and peerless engraver, Peter Simcich, so I put it off again until the premiere was guaranteed.

Finally, in 2003, Lyric Opera Kansas City's general director, Evan Luskin, and artistic director, Ward Holmquist, asked to commission the work. We came to an agreement to premiere *John Brown* in 2006 as one of the events that would celebrate the opening of Kansas City's new performing-arts center. I implemented the extensive revisions and cut still another ten minutes from the score. But delays in construction of the arts center caused the date of the premiere to be moved to May 3, 2008, which would coincide with the fiftieth anniversary of the company. It would be another four years before the arts center was ready, however, so the premiere was given in the old opera house.

All the work and disappointments were forgotten. Lyric Opera Kansas City gave *John Brown* a magnificent send-off. Maestro Holmquist conducted with eloquence and passion; Director Kristine McIntyre splendidly developed the characters and handled the large crowd scenes masterfully. The principal roles couldn't have been better cast: James Maddalena as Brown, Donnie Ray Albert as Douglass. As delighted as I was with the production, perhaps an even greater satisfaction—because it was so surprising—was the reception of the work by the audiences at all five performances.

I had worried about this. Opera audiences in the United States have been notoriously older and more conservative than the general public. What's more, Kansas City, Missouri, is where the Bible Belt meets the Old Confederacy; there are still many people in both Kansas and Missouri who were taught all their lives to hate John Brown. I had hoped that my opera would help dispel the myths and ignorance about the real man, but because I remembered the statement, "he was not a very nice man," I was not sanguine.

I needn't have worried. "In Lyric Opera's fifty-year history, there have never been such sustained standing ovations," declared the founder and former artistic director of the company, Russell Patterson, who had been the first to propose the *John Brown* premiere. Three of the reviewers predicted a long life for what one writer said "may well be the great American opera."

But my hopes for a series of productions by other companies—as had happened with *Tartuffe*—were dashed by the collapse of the economy. Looking ahead to better times, however, I spent the following summer making revisions. The general consensus, even among my friends and well-disposed critics, was that the thirteen-minute Concord scene at the end of Act II was an anti-climax and should be removed. I eventually took their advice and reduced the running time of the opera to two hours, seven minutes, but it was a painful decision. I had wanted the audience to see Brown supported by Emerson and Thoreau, giving the lie to one of the myths about the man—that he was a loner without any legitimate backing. In the end, however, I had to admit that drama and the musical form trumped historical scope.

In the preface to his Brown biography, Stephen Oates wrote that he "sought to show why Brown performed his controversial deeds rather than to damn or praise him." I followed his example in the hope that the addition of music would bring this drama to life in a new and cathartic way. As I state in my afterword (appendix 2), "For all my concern with history and drama, I am acutely aware that an opera lives or dies by the quality of its music. Here I gladly give up words and turn over the consideration of that enigmatic and timeless old man to the hearts and minds of my listeners."

20

INTERMEZZO

What Is American Opera?

Before moving on, I want to discuss some structural problems in the American opera world that make it unnecessarily difficult for successful new operas to enter the repertoire. My failure to get a production of *John Brown* during the 1990s and in the early years of this century was a great disappointment, and might have been worse had not *Tartuffe* been such a remarkable success. But paradoxically, that made the disappointment still harder to bear. When a first opera is a big hit, shouldn't that open doors for a second? In nineteenth- and early twentieth-century Europe, a successful premiere was immediately followed by productions in dozens of other cities and by commissions for future operas. Companies today, however, plan their seasons years in advance, allowing little flexibility for this kind of follow-up.

In 1983, Opera America, the national service association of professional companies, asked me to write a chapter for a book called *Perspectives: Creating and Producing Contemporary Opera and Musical Theater.* My perspective was that of the frustrated composer described above. My article, "An American Opera Network," described a plan to set up a consortium of regional companies for the express purpose of producing each year one opera whose premiere had been exceptionally successful. This would be presented in each city of the consortium. Someone at Opera America must have thought it was a good idea: the article was reprinted (with a different title) in OA's *Encore* magazine in 1999. Nevertheless, an American Opera Network remains just an idea.

If it seems that I am saying *Tartuffe* was a great success, and at the same time complaining that it was not successful enough, I must explain a few things about both the opera world and the publishing industry. Yes, *Tartuffe* is probably the most-performed full-length American opera written in the last half-century (but certainly not the most famous, nor the one seen by the largest audience). It has had some four hundred performances in six countries. If you are an opera fan and never heard of it, that's because most of its performances have been by universities and conservatories (which are not counted by Opera America or by those who compile statistics), and by foreign and small professional companies. In spite of exceptional reviews over three decades by opera magazines and major newspapers, it is not produced by the larger regional companies it was written for.

As I noted earlier, this is partly due to the mistaken belief that it is only a chamber opera, but perhaps there is also a prejudice against new *comic* operas. If you want comedy you go to a musical; most new operas are *very serious*. Has the Met ever done an American comic opera? If that ever happens, it will be the beginning of a new era: Americans will discover that modern operas can actually be entertaining! Wonder of wonders! The perennial box-office success of *The Marriage of Figaro, The Barber of Seville, Don Pasquale,* and *The Elixir of Love* reveals something about opera audiences that seems to have escaped the notice of opera impresarios. Do they not know that, according to Opera America, approximately 40 percent of the top twenty operas performed in North America are comic operas? So why is there such reluctance to produce a highly successful *American* comic opera? Is this just an example of how impresarios guard their prestige, their reputation of not "pandering to the audience"? (And yet they'll bring in a Broadway hit when they're afraid the audience is getting tired of the same old operas.) I am obviously not a neutral observer of this prejudice against comic operas. I have two dogs in this race. The premiere of *The Rivals* in 2011 was even more successful than *Tartuffe*'s, but we are already finding the same reluctance of professional companies to take on a comedy.

❀ ❀ ❀

I must also touch upon the problems of music publishers. They have been hit hard not only by the recession, but also by the explosion of technology—copy machines, the Internet, and computer programs that make music engraving a do-it-yourself project. Copyrights are often ignored in many areas of music distribution, and in almost every case, publishers and composers lose a source of revenue. Many smaller publishers have disappeared, and some enterprising composers now self-publish.

My publisher—Schirmer—like many others, has had to cut back on personnel, and cannot do as much for its composers as it used to. With the company's consent, I have tried to do some promotion myself, even though many opera impresarios automatically throw away letters from composers. I wrote directly to some of the major opera companies. Although I have not been very successful, I think my letter to the Metropolitan Opera may amuse you. It was not the usual brief invitation to consider a new opera; it was more like throwing down the gauntlet.

January 4, 2007

Dear Mr. Gelb:

I have just read the disappointing reviews for *The First Emperor*. Even though this opera was planned before your time, perhaps you should view its failure as a wake-up call for the Met to do something revolutionary.

It is not revolutionary to start with a composer who has never written a successful opera; the Met has tried that before with predictable results.

It is not revolutionary to choose a contemporary theme for yet another "CNN opera." Or to make one more fruitless stab at "fusion" music, hoping to draw in fans of both pop and classics but satisfying neither.

So what *would* be revolutionary? It would be the antithesis of all the above. What if you would commission a new work by a composer whose first opera has had hundreds of performances in multiple countries with glorious reviews and "frenetic audience response"? What if the commissioned opera were based upon the most beloved novel in the English language, one that nobody has ever dared make into an opera, despite its often-filmed romantic story, strong characters, humor, and opportunities for dances, ensembles, and passionate music? What if it were "a work of substance and theatrical energy" with "sparkling, inventive contemporary music," "melodies you can sing," and "glittering orchestration"?

Disgraceful, right? A self-respecting, progressive opera director would be out of his mind to commission an opera with such old-fashioned virtues! Think of the affront to music directors and critics who must prove to their colleagues what serious music they champion! It would be almost—well, revolutionary.

The shameless quotations I have just used to describe the new opera were all written by critics about my first opera, *Tartuffe* (see reviews on G. Schirmer's website), and I trust that they will apply to the one I am working on now, *Pride and Prejudice*, based on the Jane Austen novel. It is in two acts, and will run a little over two hours. Act I had a very successful workshop last spring.

With all best wishes for your tenure at the Met.

Surprisingly, the letter did catch the attention of Mr. Gelb. He directed the Met's dramaturg, Paul Cremo, to request the scores. Four months later I received this note from Mr. Cremo: "Thank you for sharing *Pride and Prejudice* with us. It's a beloved subject and you've done a lovely job with it, but unfortunately, we feel it isn't right for the Met at this time."

* * *

I discussed this with a friend who plays in the Met orchestra. I told her that in the early stages of *John Brown*'s composition—fifteen years earlier—I had sent a recording of its excerpts to Ken Noda, assistant to music director James Levine and a well-known musician in his own right. Ken was so moved by the work that he immediately phoned me and asked for a preliminary score. Months later he gave me the news that the Met wasn't interested.

I wanted to know why, in my orchestra friend's opinion, the Met commissions only new works that are "cutting-edge" and often ugly. She shrugged; mine was obviously a question she had heard before. "It's all about prestige," she said. "Such conductors think difficult, challenging works prove their intellectual prowess. If they perform a beautiful or entertaining new work, they're afraid the critics will say they have given in to the box office."

I can understand that. I have occasionally been accused of "writing down" to the public. I usually reply, "No, I'm writing *up* to a public that loves Mozart, Verdi, Puccini, and Gershwin as much as I do. If, in my own language, I can satisfy *that* audience, I have achieved something far more difficult and important than trying to reinvent music."

✿ ✿ ✿

Opera in America has changed in my lifetime. The question I am most often asked goes something like this: "Isn't musical theater, in the Broadway sense, really the opera of our time?"

True, it may be getting closer to opera in *form*—some musicals have little or no spoken dialogue—but it has miles to go. Why? Because of the music. Even the best of Broadway musicals still rely heavily on musical clichés and production formulas, and are aimed at a different level of musicality. Many opera lovers consider them another species, even when they enjoy them as light entertainment. If you believe that opera and musical theater are the same thing, please name a Broadway show as emotionally powerful as *Otello* or *Jenufa*, as entertaining musically as *Meistersinger* or *Figaro*, or that has singing and orchestral music of such scope, beauty, power, or grace as these and many other operas—then we'll talk about comparisons.

"Well and good," you might say, "but a good new musical is still better than a bad new opera." I agree and admit that some of the classic musicals are more entertaining than most operas written in my lifetime. I was reminded of this just the other day when I was watching video clips on the Classic Arts Channel. First I saw a boring scene by a celebrated modern composer. The music was labored and mannered— an example of how easily "prestigious" can slide into "pretentious." A short time later came a clip of three scenes from Lerner and Loewe's *My Fair Lady*. They were charming, witty, and full of good-humored tunes.

I think it's the latter—good melodies in which the music perfectly fits the words—that audiences miss the most in new operas. I can't understand why so many otherwise-skillful composers turn words into anti-melodies that leap all over the staff in unexpected ways, bearing no resemblance to the meaning or the rhythm of the words. Too many composers are still afraid of those critics or colleagues who deplore any "conventional" style in a new opera. But usually the *style* isn't the problem at all. What's lacking is character and *musical* drama.

Many twenty-first-century operas have interesting stories, accessible music, and two things that used to give musicals an advantage over opera: brilliant staging and—since the advent of supertitles—comprehensible words. But titles have brought an unexpected consequence: operas are becoming more like movies. For opera lovers, this is not good news.

I have recently seen several new operas in spectacular productions. The cost of the scenic hardware alone must have been in the hundreds of thousands of dollars. Each was a visual cornucopia. Isn't that what we want? Can anyone doubt that we have become primarily a visual society? Perhaps that's why I heard a member of the audience at one of these operas remark, "It sounds like movie music."

Now movie music can be effective or not, but it has always been quite different from opera music. Movie music is "background music"; in opera, music is the foreground. Opera aficionados in America loved operas even when they couldn't understand the language in which the operas were being sung. *Prima la musica, poi le parole.* As Mozart put it in a letter he wrote in 1781: "In an opera the poetry must be altogether the obedient daughter of the music. Why are Italian comic operas popular everywhere . . . even in Paris? . . . Just because there the music reigns supreme" (translation by Emily Anderson).

When first introduced, supertitles brought larger audiences—that was good. But I grant the point made by many traditionalists: Titles can lead to lazy pronunciation by singers and to overloaded orchestration by composers. But what bothers me in some recent operas is more subtle and more damaging than these easily avoidable problems. It is the lack of integrity of musical form, which has ceded its supremacy to dramatic continuity.

What I'm lamenting is that musical form is rarely being used to organize entire scenes. While I'm not claiming that every situation in opera can be treated this way, think of the beginning of *La Bohème*. Those four quick little notes and the melodies that grow from them run through the entire scene, giving way sometimes to other more lyrical melodies, then reappearing in different forms—just as the principal melodies in a symphony give way to a contrasting section, to transitional material, and are developed and recapitulated. In opera this is done more freely, and we feel great satisfaction in experiencing this musical

journey, even though we might not realize how persuasively it is organizing the drama.

Puccini, no doubt, learned about operatic form from Verdi, a master
of the technique I have described (see the first scene of *Falstaff*, for
instance), or from Mozart (see the great Act 2 Finale of *Figaro*, which
through four scenes carries out motivic development and key relationships as if Mozart were writing a symphony). Indeed, this kind of musical organization was used by *every* good opera composer for at least two
centuries. One of my favorite examples is the Finale of Act I of *The
Barber of Seville: "Ehi di casa, buona gente!"* No character ever sings
the orchestral melody that first accompanies Almaviva disguised as a
soldier, but that accompaniment is the glue that holds together the
entire scene. It is the principal motif, alternating with other melodies
and motifs, that guides the scene through recitative, comedy, coloratura, all kinds of other adventures, and is finally recapitulated to ignite
one of those fabulous Rossini ensembles.

Here's another way of stating this same principle: opera—from its
inception—has been constructed as a series of musical scenes. When I
was worrying about how I could possibly turn the beloved but very long
novel *Pride and Prejudice* into an opera, I happened to see a performance of Tchaikovsky's *Eugene Onegin*, and was reminded that instead
of calling it an opera, Tchaikovsky used the subtitle "Lyric Scenes." I
suddenly realized that in a sense, this is what all good operas are. They
are episodic. Opera audiences don't require back stories or detailed
explanations of plot; they want music that "cuts to the chase"—which in
opera means to the *emotion*. Verdi omitted almost the entire first act of
Shakespeare's *Othello* in his opera; do we miss it? I don't; in fact, when
I see the play now, I am impatient with that act, and in the rest of the
play I miss Verdi's music.

✸ ✸ ✸

In my article "The Text Trap" (appendix A), I advised young choral
composers not to let the words bully them into slavish obedience. "How
often," I wrote, "after hearing a new setting, have we come away with
the impression that the composer simply set the poem one line after
another with no over-all musical plan? This is not composition; this is a
catalog of musical ideas: six melodies in search of a composition."

"New operas," I added, "often have the same problem. It seems that
the producer, the director or the librettist has bullied the composer into

abdicating his/her age-old right to be in charge—to compose an opera with dramatic *musical* forms. Here, too, we often end up with a parade of isolated ideas without any substantial musical satisfaction. Great operas have been written to mediocre texts; none have been written with fragmentary music."

Impresarios can spend millions on scenic splendor, supertitles can make the drama more explicit, but nothing will make audiences *love* new operas except beautiful, animated, and powerful music. *Music* must tell the story and make you *feel* it in your heart. Fortunately, some composers are re-learning this basic truth. Jake Heggie's *Dead Man Walking* is a good example. A poignant story by Sister Helen Prejean, an operatically savvy libretto by a fine playwright, Terence McNally, and music by a composer with a gift for melody and drama all combined to produce a gripping and moving opera, premiered by the San Francisco Opera in 2000. Kenneth Puts also has a gift for melody and drama; his *Silent Night* was premiered by the Minnesota Opera in 2011. One patron at a subsequent production was heard to remark, "Well, it's safe to go to new operas again!" The tide indeed is turning: both operas are receiving many further productions, and *Silent Night* even won the Pulitzer Prize for music.

Supertitles were probably not necessary for *Dead Man Walking*, though they were used. They are most valuable for operas sung in languages foreign to the audience (*Silent Night* is in several languages, an ideal context for supertitles). But for operas in the audience's own language, supertitles clearly share the blame for this shift in importance from music to the story. When the audience is dividing its attention between reading the titles and looking at the stage, it has little concentration left for the music. Watching an opera can become very much like watching a movie—the music is in the background. A disturbing but predictable result of this reversal is that some audience members no longer care if the music is mediocre or even bad, so long as it has some obvious connection with the action. They are so busy following the drama, they hardly hear the music. But if you only want a *story*, why go to the opera at all? Movies are much cheaper.

21

RUSSIAN EXTRAVAGANZA

Those disappointing years trying to find a home for *John Brown* were alleviated by some invigorating experiences: dozens of successful productions of *Tartuffe*, international travel for both symphonic and opera productions, and, as previously noted, the composition of a new opera. (You will meet Mrs. Malaprop and *The Rivals* in chapter 23.)

I was not able to attend the first two foreign performances of *Tartuffe*. The first was by the University of British Columbia in 1988; the second, in Chinese, by Xiamen University, China, in 1995. Overlapping those two were three trips to Russia.

I met the late Irina Arkhipova, the legendary Bolshoi Opera mezzo, in San Francisco in 1989. She brought five of the best young Soviet singers (including Dmitri Hvorostovsky) to the United States to join five young American singers in a series of concerts called "Arias for Peace." The project was under the auspices of Beyond War, the national organization Donata was active in; I was their musical advisor. Irina stayed in our house for ten days, off and on—days remembered not only for the excitement of the events, but also for the language difficulties. Neither Doe nor I had learned much Russian yet, Irina spoke a bit of German and less English, so we communicated mostly in bad Italian with snatches of French and whatever came to hand.

As becomes a gracious house guest, Irina asked to hear some of my music. I played a recording of "Fair Robin I Love," from *Tartuffe*, which she liked, and an aria from *John Brown*, sung by Deborah Voigt, "These Wooded Streams," after which she said, "We haven't had such a beautiful aria written in Russia since the war." (Thank you, Debbie.) Irina invited me to come to Moscow the following year as a judge for the Tchaikovsky International Vocal Competition. I had learned from experience that I do not like to be a judge, so I politely declined. "In that case," she said, "won't you come and be the competition's guest of honor?" As Doe was invited to come too, we gratefully accepted.

At the end of June 1990, we flew to Moscow, where we were put up at the Ukraina Hotel and given a translator, Alexander Pokonov, a tall, affable young man with a full head of black hair and a chinstrap beard. Doe and I had tried to learn some Russian before coming, but we would have been lost without Alex. The competition was held in the most beautiful hall in Moscow, the Hall of Columns, and as it turned out, the winner was our friend Deborah Voigt. (I did not tell Irina that she had already heard Debbie's voice on a recording. She had no idea that we were acquainted.)

One of the most thrilling events of our stay took place at Tchaikovsky's country house in Klin, about fifty miles northwest of Moscow. Each year the competition is given, the participants plant a tree on Tchaikovsky's estate. This year, as guest of honor, it was my privilege to shovel the first bit of dirt onto the newly planted tree, an event shown on Russian television. As I acquitted myself of this honor, I couldn't help wondering, *Whatever in the world am I doing here?*

On our second day in Moscow, Irina introduced me to the conductor of the USSR Large Radio-Television Concert Orchestra, Murad Kazhlayev. He was an ebullient, enthusiastic man with a pleasant, round face. He was from Dagestan, and we would eventually get to know him and his family well. He took me to lunch at the Composers' Union. A Bay-Area filmmaker working in Moscow had brought him recordings and scores of my symphonic works, and Murad proposed a full concert of these with his orchestra the following season. It would be in the Hall of Columns, he said, and asked if I could come. Of course I accepted. He said it would be the first time a Russian orchestra had devoted an entire symphonic concert to a living American composer. He invited us to hear his orchestra in their recording home the next day.

We were taken to a state-of-the-art studio. There were seats for a small audience, but the room—made of resplendent wood—was designed for broadcasts and recording; each orchestral section had its own microphone. Murad gave us a private mini-concert. It was breathtaking in its brilliance and accuracy. I was most struck by Shostakovich's light-hearted *Festive Overture*—so very different from his symphonies.

Later I learned that Murad was a fan of American jazz. He played me his own jazz orchestra's transcriptions of big-band music that he had copied by ear from pirated recordings. They sounded almost identical to the originals. (I love big-band music, as well as bluegrass, good jazz, and Sousa marches; they are to America what Strauss waltzes are to Vienna.)

It was decided that the all-Mechem concert would take place March 30 the following year. When we came home, Doe enrolled in a Russian course at San Francisco State University and I tried to teach myself the language by the Assimil method, which included cassette recordings of conversations. I wrote a few commissioned choral works, but spent most of my time on the composition of *John Brown*.

* * *

A year later, March 1991, Moscow was very different. There was snow, of course, but it was thawing—and so was the Cold War atmosphere in the USSR. With Gorbachev had come glasnost, the opening up of certain freedoms. There were demonstrations in the streets, for and against these changes. Although we were happy to see the mitigation of so much harshness in Soviet society, it was a blow to my concert. Because Russians were for the first time allowed to emigrate, Murad had lost nearly all his first-chair players, and a few others as well, to European and other foreign orchestras.

Murad had asked me to select an American conductor for the concert—someone familiar with my music. My friend Corrick Brown was the only conductor who had performed both symphonies as well as the Jayhawk Overture, and he gladly accepted the offer. It was a pleasure to have Corrick and his pianist wife, Norma, with us; they were both old friends since our days together at Stanford and Vienna. Irina Arkhipova agreed to sing three of my songs. The orchestra was still a good one, rehearsals went well, and Melodiya Records intended to produce a CD of the symphonic works. But suddenly Moscow was hit by an outbreak of influenza.

Substitute players began showing up at the final rehearsals, and even at the concert we saw several players for the first time. Irina caught the bug, too, but sang effectively in spite of a fever and sore throat. Despite all, the concert went well and was received enthusiastically by the audience and by the Shostakovich expert, Manushir Yakubov, who gave the concert a glowing review in the *Musical Observer* of Moscow.

The recording, however, was disappointing. Evidently, permission to record had been denied by some Soviet bureaucrat at the last minute, so a Melodiya engineer (a friend of Murad) was hidden at the back of the balcony and made an unauthorized recording. Although it was done with state-of-the-art equipment, it yielded a significantly different sound from those made in the orchestra's studio. When ten violins are recorded with a dedicated microphone, the engineer can make them sound like sixteen. But on this recording, they still sound like ten and do not balance the large wind, brass, and percussion sections, particularly as some of the players were substitutes. The balance is so unpredictable that an oboe or horn subsidiary part sometimes jumps out as if it were the principal melody.

When I heard the playback at the Melodiya office, I thought it would be better not to release a CD. Corrick disagreed, and so did the executives of the company, so I reluctantly gave in. By the time it was released, the name of the company had become Russian Disc. I prefer the recordings I have by American orchestras, but they are not available commercially.

None of this, however, could diminish the excitement of our adventure. Doe and our three daughters were present (our son couldn't get off work) and reveled in all the attention. A day or two after the concert, Katie took a trip to see friends in Europe, but Liz and Jenni joined us and the Kazhlayhevs on a two-day train trip to Makhachkala, capital of Dagestan on the Caspian Sea. That was Murad's principal home, where he was a hero. He not only was a popular conductor throughout Russia, but also had written the scores for some forty films. (Even when he came to visit us in San Francisco, the Russian clerk at the local Radio Shack recognized him immediately.) Murad had arranged for a Dagestan television crew to meet our train and interview me later, in the studio. He insisted that I speak Russian, even though the ubiquitous Alex was right there beside us. It must have been the slowest interview on record.

Later, the ever-generous Murad took us on a couple of fascinating excursions. The first (complete with TV crew) was to the ancient fortress of Derbent, on the Caspian Sea, just north of the Azerbaijani border. We saw archaeological structures over five thousand years old.

Even more interesting was the drive through the Caucasus Mountains, across Chechnya through Pyatigorsk to Kislovodsk, the most beautiful spa city in Southern Russia, where Rachmaninoff had a summer house. At the Philharmonia Museum the curator asked me to play the great composer's piano. I'd like to be able to say that I sat down and rattled off one of Rachmaninoff's *Moments Musicaux*, but my meager technique and bad memory reduced my "performance" to improvisations.

We flew back to Moscow from Nalchik after another formidable banquet given by some of that city's music aristocracy. Finally, three weeks after leaving San Francisco, we flew home.

Later that same year, Murad visited us in San Francisco. He had been invited by Corrick to conduct his music with the Santa Rosa Symphony Orchestra. Around Thanksgiving, 1991, he came with Valida, their son Hadji-Murat, and, of course, Alex. In addition to some of his own ballet music, Murad conducted the Khachaturian piano concerto with Roy Bogas as soloist. His conducting was as vivid and colorful as his music. It was a delightful visit; after the concert they stayed with us for about a week, marveling at American abundance, especially the electronic gadgetry, some of which they bought.

* * *

The third trip to Russia, for the Russian-language premiere of *Tartuffe* in 1996, came about in a surprising way. A Russian pianist living in the Bay Area, Dora Zhibitskaya, saw the 1993 Opera San Jose production and recommended the opera to the Mussorgsky National Opera in St. Petersburg, where she had once been a house pianist. Stanislav Gaudassinski, the artistic and general director, faxed me that the company would like to perform the opera in the spring of 1996. He said the Russian translation and the scenic planning were already underway.

He wrote again the next year and asked if there was any possibility of getting sponsorship from an American corporation. The opera company's government subsidy had been greatly reduced. I answered that corporations in the United States often supported the arts because such gifts are tax-deductible, but I doubted that a subsidy to a foreign institution would qualify. But then I remembered something that had come up after our last trip to Moscow.

When conductor Corrick Brown had told an old Stanford friend how much it cost us to travel to Moscow, his friend answered, "Why didn't you let me know in advance? Our foundation has money specifically for supporting American music abroad." Corrick's friend was Harold Kant, who managed the Rex Foundation, the charitable arm of the Grateful Dead, one of the most popular and most musical of American rock bands. I talked to Mr. Kant, who was indeed interested, and the band members approved a gift of ten thousand dollars to the opera company for the *Tartuffe* production. Because of the sudden economic downturn in Russia, that gift may have saved the production from being canceled.

This was an even bigger deal for my son, Ed, than for me. He had been a great fan of the band—a "Deadhead"—for years, and he was hugely proud that they had helped get his dad's opera produced in Russia. It also raised my status in his eyes when Hal Kant reported that the players said, "Yeah, we know Kirke Mechem's music. Project approved." I had occasionally run into Jerry Garcia when he was just getting started. We both hung around the Golden Gate Park tennis courts in the 1960s when my symphonies were being premiered by Krips.

There was another delay, but finally the premiere was set for October 30, 1996. The official name of the company was the Saint Petersburg Mussorgsky State Opera and Ballet Theatre, but people still referred to it as the *Maly*. That means "small," to distinguish it from the larger Mariinsky Theatre. Small it is not. It is the company that gave the premieres of Prokofiev's *War and Peace* and Shostakovich's *Lady Macbeth of Mzensk*. It is a block-long complex that houses a large symphony orchestra and chorus, a ballet troupe, scenic-design and costume studios, a restaurant, and a group of apartments—all requiring a staff of eight hundred. (In 2007 the theater returned to its original name, the Mikhailovsky.)

* * *

Journal, November 9, 1996: We got back last Tuesday evening, and I am still fighting jet lag, though Doe seems to adjust almost immediately. The trip exceeded our expectations in every way. Even the weather wasn't nearly as bad as we had prepared for. The performance (in Russian) was terrific and a hit with the St. Petersburg audience. The translation must have been excellent because the audience laughed at all the right places. The theater was a large one and I was gratified that the original orchestration was used so successfully. Gaudassinski says it will be shown on television all over Russia, kept in the repertory for three years, and probably will be taken on several international tours. We had our own two-bedroom, two-bath apartment adjoining the theater, plus our own translator/ guide, meals, and seats in the czar's box for the company's performances of five or six other ballets and operas. (They give more than 300 performances a year!) The first time I heard a run-through of *Tartuffe*, sitting up there in that Imperial box, I said to Doe, "My God, I've written a Russian opera!" How strange that the language so affects the sound of the music. The conductor was Evgeny Perunov; the stage director, Andrey Bashlovkin. With some of the Grateful Dead's money they bought a revolving stage, used for the first time in this production.

At seven o'clock on the morning of the premiere we heard a banging on the door of our apartment. Soaking wet from a downpour, in came Murad Kazhlayev, exuberant as ever. He had taken the night train from Moscow—a complete surprise to us. That made the premiere all the more fun. He knew many of the people at the theater, as they had premiered an opera of his some years before.

❋ ❋ ❋

Unfortunately, the company's European tours and many of their other grand plans for *Tartuffe* were greatly curtailed. The Russian financial crisis worsened the next year, culminating in 1998, when the government devalued the ruble and defaulted on its debt.

Learning the Russian language was a stimulating bonus to these trips. Of course we never became as fluent as we were in German after living three years in Vienna, but to be able to read and converse at all in what seemed a mysterious, exotic language was a thrill. I had always loved Russian music, literature, and theater. I'm sorry to say that I still can't read Tolstoy or Chekhov in the original, but at least I have more feeling for the language and the culture than I had before. Unfortunately, seventy years of Soviet totalitarian misery had left Russia in such a sorry state, it was hard to reconcile those days of cultural glory with the disorder we saw everywhere.

22

TARTUFFE SPRICHT DEUTSCH

We will never forget the next European *Tartuffe* because of its date. It was produced in Germany by Opera Hagen, in Rhine-Westphalia. Our Lufthansa flight left San Francisco on the afternoon of September 10, 2001; from Frankfurt we traveled by train to Hagen on the afternoon of 9/11. Our taxi driver in Hagen was the first to tell us of the planes crashing into the World Trade Center. We turned on the television in our hotel room and were horrified, frightened, but relieved that our daughter Liz and family had moved away from Tribeca the first of the month; their old apartment had been close to the towers. We tried to phone, but the international lines were clogged. A little later, while we were out, Liz called and left a message that they were all right. Our son in California phoned us, filled us in on the attacks, and said he would call Liz to explain why we had not been able to reach her.

Uta Schmidtsdorff, the *Dramaturgin* at Opera Hagen, had been my correspondent in making arrangements for the visit, and continued to be helpful while we were in Hagen. The city itself is unprepossessing; it looks more like a small town than a city of two hundred thousand. We learned that it comprises five hilly boroughs, in the middle of which is the flat river valley where the center of town lies. The stately opera house is the center of the city; our hotel and the train station were within walking distance.

On the second day, Uta brought me to the office of general director Rainer Friedemann, who had called a meeting of the staff. They wanted to ask me—in the presence of a reporter who had brought up the subject in his newspaper—if the premiere should be called off because of the terrorist attacks. It was a somber and emotional conversation. All were in agreement that September 11 had been a pivotal moment in world history, a boundary over which humanity had stepped, and that it was not just America's problem but would have serious, worldwide consequences. I said that I expected our government to use restraint and avoid stigmatizing all Muslims. The reporter and opera people were glad to hear me say this. They feared what President Bush might do. I said that in regard to canceling the premiere Saturday, I would fully support whatever Herr Friedemann decided. Eventually, influenced partly by reading that the New York City Opera was resuming its performances with a comic opera on Friday, the opera staff decided not to cancel.

We took three or four long walks in the surrounding wooded hills. They provided a much-needed respite of natural beauty in this supercharged atmosphere. We treasure the memory of a lunch in a friendly *Gasthaus* in the woods. A welcome bonus to the opera production was a Thursday evening concert of my chamber music, after which I spoke and answered questions from the audience. I always enjoy this kind of interaction with the public.

We heard the first two performances, sung in Thomas Martin's German translation that is in the published vocal score. There were no supertitles and the acoustics were bad. The house was only about three-quarters full, mostly elderly people, and there was less laughter than in any other *Tartuffe* production I have seen. The terrorist attacks were undoubtedly still on people's minds. I have been told that opera audiences in Hagen have always been conservative. However, there were a couple of bilingual British singers in the cast who gave a different reason for the subdued response: they said that the German translation is nowhere near as funny as the English text. Translations seldom are.

A year later, however, *Tartuffe* would be sung in English with German titles in Vienna, and the audience would roar with laughter. But how can you compare the good burghers of a sleepy North German town with the fun-loving Viennese? The surprising thing about the Hagen production was that the reviews were so good. The company took its production on tour to a couple of other German cities.

I will spare you the travelogue of our remaining ten days in Germany. Fascinating as Berlin, Leipzig, Dresden, and Weimar were to us, I will skip to April the following year for one of the happiest musical experiences of my life.

* * *

The *Wiener Kammeroper* (Vienna Chamber Opera), in its 2001–2002 season, had begun a series called "Twentieth-Century Classics." *Tartuffe* was their first offering in this series, and I was invited to participate in its production. (Yes, even the Viennese thought my work was a chamber opera; they used the reduced orchestration.) You can imagine what a thrill it was for me. As a bedazzled young man in Vienna over forty years before, who only *hoped* to become a composer, I never dreamed that I would hear my own opera performed there.

Our good friends Ewald and Christl Winkler picked us up at the airport and took us to the Hotel Post (where Mozart and Wagner had stayed). When we opened the windows in our hotel room, we heard an aria from *Tartuffe* being sung across the courtyard. The next day I went to Doblinger's music store to see if they had Schirmer's libretto of my opera; I wanted to give copies to Viennese friends. It was in the display window. The *Kammeroper*'s production was excellent, and the reviews were glorious. For a Kansas boy who never saw an opera growing up, this was a fairy tale.

Many of our old friends were still in Vienna to celebrate with us. Particularly dear to us was the presence of Philippe and Cynthia Dunoyer, who came from Paris. They had traveled from Paris to the San Francisco premiere in 1980, and this was just as joyous a reunion. Walking through the old inner city, having lunch in small restaurants we had remembered (the Dunoyers had also lived in Vienna a couple of years), enjoying *Ausflüge* to the Vienna woods and to Baden with Felice Schediwy—all this was magical. We were given front-row seats to *Die Meistersinger* at the *Staatsoper*, free tickets to the *Philharmoniker* concert, and visited the places where we had lived. Harriet Krips, Josef's widow, lived in Switzerland but came to the May 2 premiere.

The *Kammeroper* gave eighteen performances of *Tartuffe;* we stayed for the first two. The Viennese music critics are among the most feared in Europe. When we lived there in the 1960s, the best a performer from the United States could hope for was "pretty good for an American." Another phrase was applied to *any* foreign performer: "What we heard was not *our* Beethoven." But nearly every review of *Tartuffe* was positive, several reporting the "frenetic ovation." I want to quote part of Derek Weber's review in the *Salzburger Nachrichten* because it reinforces a point I have touched upon already:

Laughter Permitted in This Opera

This correspondent has rarely heard such a witty contemporary opera, carried out with such finely honed irony. . . . But it would be a mistake to write off this comically irreverent music as mere postmodern arbitrariness. . . . There is depth in it. In this country, this kind of music is not highly valued (and therefore ignored); what this chiefly reveals is that ignorant delusion of ours which values only art that leads to tragic tears. Only in sunnier cultures are tears of laughter permitted.

The writer was undoubtedly referring to Italy when he spoke of "sunnier cultures." He certainly couldn't mean the United States, where professional performances of new comic operas are as rare as they are in Austria.

23

THE RIVALS

Flatulence Will Get You Nowhere

Mrs. Malaprop was the answer to my prayers.

By 1997 *Tartuffe* had been performed nearly two hundred times, and I began to think about writing another comic opera. The still-unperformed *John Brown* seemed to be going nowhere, and I needed another big project to keep my spirits up. I wanted this new opera to be quite different from *Tartuffe*—American, if possible—one that would give me a chance to write in the lighthearted idioms of American musicals. I had grown up with the great tunes of Gershwin, Kern, and Porter, and tried to imitate them in my early songs. I liked musical comedies; in my youth I had written a couple of bad ones. But as I got to know opera better, I found the comic operas of Mozart and Rossini much more satisfying. Not only were the arias and ensembles more beautiful and musically sophisticated, but the action and theatrical humor were turned into delightful music. I had tried to follow that tradition in *Tartuffe*, but its musical style was international rather than specifically American.

I failed to discover a suitable classic American comedy, and the popular Broadway plays of the twentieth century seemed dated or otherwise not right for opera. I widened my search to include British plays that could possibly be Americanized, and hit upon Sheridan's Restoration comedy, *The Rivals*. It has a sparkling comic story and a rich variety of characters. It takes place in eighteenth-century Bath, England, where royal titles were wedded to high-society money, and it occurred to me that Newport, Rhode Island, about 1900 was not only a good American equivalent, but also just the sort of flamboyant place and period that would suit opera to a T. (I am grateful to my friend, Dottie Wexler, for pointing this out.)

In the fall of 1997 I learned that a professional theater company in Wisconsin—American Players Theatre—was performing Sheridan's play, so on the way home from Boston, Doe and I stopped in Spring Green to see if *The Rivals* could entertain a twentieth-century audience. In spite of its dated dramaturgy, the plot and characters retained their buoyancy and were greeted with laughter and applause.

On the same trip, we had visited the eighty-room "cottages" that provided evidence of the history of Newport, where the Vanderbilts, Astors, and their friends sailed, dined, and attended balls and horse races. The casino is still there. From the Newport Historical Society I obtained photographs from the Gilded Age that showed the Casino's café open to the lawn tennis court where the national championships were first played. As a former tournament player, I couldn't resist beginning one of the opera's scenes with the sound of a bouncing tennis ball. The casino was a public meeting place; it serves as one of the two stage sets in the opera, alternating with the elegant salon of Mrs. Malaprop.

This was the era of the "dollar princess," but also of her exact opposite, the "Gibson Girl," made popular in the satirical drawings of Charles Dana Gibson. She was a more independent, modern young woman who wanted nothing to do with the traditional role of a debutante—that of a husband-hunter in her own wealthy class. In Sheridan's play, the ingénue is named Lydia Languish, but as I wanted to emphasize her American modernity, I named my Gibson Girl Lydia Larkspur, a spirited young woman with no hint of languishing.

Several other characters in Sheridan's play had to change with the time and place, too. I wanted Falkland's behavior to be a pure example of the egotistical male jealousy that demands adoring, unceasing, unconditional love—impossible for any woman to achieve—so I eliminated the backstory that he had once saved Julia from drowning. He becomes the insufferable Nicholas Astor. Another transformation turns Bob Acres, Lydia's rustic suitor, into Jasper Vanderbilt, of the Kentucky Vanderbilts. (There really was a branch of that family in Kentucky.)

The character I changed the most is Sheridan's belligerent Sir Lucius O'Trigger. The stereotype of a militant bully in 1900 America was not an Irishman, but a Prussian, so Sir Lucius became the fortune hunter, Baron von Hakenbock. I also gave him an idiosyncrasy borrowed from a character in another Sheridan play, *The Duenna*: he is terrified of marrying a beautiful woman.

But how could I possibly change Sheridan's greatest character, Mrs. Malaprop, so famous that (like Tartuffe) her name has entered the dictionary. A "malapropism" is any humorous misuse of similar sounding words. You can find examples from Shakespeare (Dogberry) to Yogi Berra and George W. Bush ("Anyone engaging in illegal financial transactions will be caught and persecuted"). I used as many of Sheridan's original malapropisms as I thought appropriate, but two centuries of linguistic change have robbed many of them of their humor or meaning. I had fun trying to replace these with new inventions: "I demand a full expiration," and "Young man, flatulence will get you nowhere."

Indeed, writing this libretto and music was sheer fun, and I have been delighted that performers and audiences—even critics—have experienced it in the same spirit. Unlike Molière's *Tartuffe*, a funny but classic satire, Sheridan's *Rivals* is an unapologetic farce. Nevertheless, its humor is based on human character and folly as observed by a genius. (How else can you describe a young man of twenty-two who writes such a masterpiece?) There is abundant social satire in both the play and the opera, but at their center is a harmless, ridiculous old lady, not a lecherous swindler posing as a holy man. I have changed the play's structure and characters radically, but the ingenious plot is all Sheridan.

*   *   *

I have said before that diverse characters are crucial to me in choosing a subject for opera. I have come to believe that the main reason—perhaps the only one—for turning a play or novel into an opera is the opportunity for music to make the characters and their actions come alive in a fuller, more palpable existence. Opera is not the place for philosophy. It needs *people*. The more diverse they are, the more diverse and colorful the music can be. Music can give us the indefinable essence of a character. And once a character has been given a musical profile, the composer can vary the music as the character changes. Ever since Wagner's *Leitmotif*, good operas have often demonstrated this technique of variations on a theme, which creates a richer musical experience for the audience, especially when the opera is new. Two hours of unfamiliar music with no repetition or development is a lot to digest.

I have sometimes used musical idioms from American popular music in this work, but that does not make it a musical comedy. When I am asked what the difference between a musical and an opera is, I usually answer: musicals are for those who love theater and like music; for opera it's the other way around—it's for those who love music and like theater. But people who go to musicals love music, too—just a different kind of music. A better and shorter way of putting it is this: operas cost money; musicals make money. So if you want to call this comic opera a musical, please go right ahead. And tell all your friends.

I finished the libretto in early 1998. My original title was *The Newport Rivals;* I thought it would be obvious that the opera was based on Sheridan's play with the action shifted to Newport. I was wrong. Almost no one made that inference, so several years later I went back to Sheridan's title. The opera was tried out in three different university workshops of scenes or acts. There was also a reading of scene 1 with orchestra by the VOX program of the New York City Opera under George Manahan, and an entire concert of scenes from *The Rivals* and *John Brown* by the San Francisco Lyric Chorus. (This group and its fine conductor, Robert Gurney, have given many local premieres of my choral work.) The first public production of both acts of *The Rivals*, with two pianos, was given by the graduate students at the University of Maryland in November 2005. It was produced and directed by Leon Major, conducted by Miah Im, and though costumes and scenery were minimal, it was one of the most imaginative and musically impressive university productions I have seen of any opera.

Still, it took six more years before *The Rivals* received its professional premiere with orchestra in September 2011. (Do you hear a leitmotif playing here?) It was worth waiting for: Skylight Opera Theatre, Milwaukee—under the artistic leadership of Bill Theisen—made it an "instant classic," according to one of the reviews. As I told the director, Dorothy Danner, and the conductor, Richard Carsey, the production was so brilliant, I have no idea how good the opera itself is. But a couple of years later, when the Bronx Opera gave the East Coast premiere, the ticket sales and praise by the New York critics gave me hope that *The Rivals* would ultimately be as successful as *Tartuffe*. As noted before, audiences rarely get a chance to laugh at a new opera.

24

DARCY SINGS

Pride and Prejudice

Perhaps the delays in getting my first three operas produced should have cooled my enthusiasm for composing in that genre, but all three enjoyed remarkable success. In hindsight, it seems to me that my earlier compositions—songs, works for chorus, and orchestra and chamber ensembles—were all a preparation for writing opera. I do not expect to be remembered for my symphonies or chamber music, but have reason to hope that my four operas will find a place in the repertoire, as have many of my choral works.

In fairness to my instrumental works, however, I must add that although the zeitgeist was not kind to them, *audiences* preferred them to the more "advanced" works. Now that critics and younger composers are again welcoming tonality, I am curious to know how my symphonies and chamber music will fare with today's audiences. The few that have been tried recently have been surprisingly successful.

Be that as it may, when the composition of *The Rivals* was finished and the usual long wait for its premiere began to depress me, I knew that only by composing a new opera could I renew my spirit. Once more I began to search for the right subject. For my fourth (and probably final) opera I had my heart set on finding a play or novel with a great love story, one that also offered the variety of characters and situations I always look for. Additionally, I hoped my source would be an American work, preferably from the Midwest, where I grew up. But several months' reading turned up nothing I thought I could turn into a good opera.

Then I happened to see the 1940 *Pride and Prejudice* film—the one with Laurence Olivier and Greer Garson—and a bell rang in my brain. I did not like that adaptation at all, but it reminded me of how much I loved the book. I immediately read it again and was delighted to find how theatrically Jane Austen set up her scenes. I later learned that her family and friends regularly produced plays at home. (One of the first was *The Rivals*.) I realized that *Pride and Prejudice* satisfied all my requirements except that it was set in small-town England, not Mid-America. I briefly considered transferring the story to America, but quickly realized that would be a great mistake. Can you imagine Darcy as a Kansas cattle baron? (I shudder to think I may be giving some "concept" director an appalling idea.)

To compress four hundred pages of words into two hours of music is daunting. The 1995 television version ran over five hours. My project was so formidable, in fact, that I told no one but Doe about it until I had written several scenarios, gradually whittling them down to workable size. I then held readings of several provisional librettos until I thought I had achieved one short enough to leave room for music. And now that the work is finished, I fear that hardcore *Pride and Prejudice* fans—there are millions of them—will not forgive me.

I apologize in advance for the necessary cuts, for the telescoping of scenes and characters and for the occasional rearrangement of locales: in the opera there are only three Bennet daughters, not five, and the first scene does not begin at the Bennets' house or even at the first assembly. In order to get the action moving quickly, the opera opens with the ball at Netherfield. I have tried to arrange all this so that the important words and actions occur in the same order as in the novel. I use Jane Austen's own words wherever possible, only making changes necessary for modern comprehension, brevity, or for musical reasons. I also put some of the choral passages into verse. The chorus represents the townspeople and friends of the Bennets, and gives voice to some of Jane Austen's narration.

In spite of these changes, however, I want to assure fans of the novel that I love it as much as they do, and have tried my best to remain true to its characters and story. I sorely regret the cuts I had to make, but please remember—only Wagner could get away with five-hour operas.

I am encouraged by the enthusiastic response from members of the Jane Austen Society, who attended some of the preliminary workshops of the opera.

In the meantime, I have discovered that there are actually two or three people on this planet who don't like Jane Austen's novel! They have asked me such questions as, "Why write an opera on *Pride and Prejudice?* After all the films, plays, and books, who needs an operatic version?" I can answer these questions only with a more difficult question: "Why has no one written an opera on *Pride and Prejudice* before?"

It is the most beloved novel in the English language; it has strong and varied characters, humor, opportunities for dancing, for ensembles and scenic beauty, and above all, it is built around one of the most fascinating love stories of all time. These are the hallmarks of opera. While films have the technique to open up action in ways the stage cannot, opera can more powerfully represent the passions and nuances of human emotions. The language of love is music.

Why then, for two centuries, was *Pride and Prejudice* overlooked by opera composers? Could it be because the soprano doesn't die? In nineteenth-century opera that seems to have been obligatory, except in comic operas, which *Pride and Prejudice* could never have become. In spite of its frequent irony, the book has important scenes of anguish and even anger. As Somerset Maugham observed in naming *Pride and Prejudice* one of the world's ten greatest novels, Austen "had too much common sense and too sprightly a humor to be a romantic."

But what about twentieth-century English composers? Britten, the most prolific, was interested mainly in the uncommon. "Austen was interested in the common," Maugham wrote. "She made it uncommon by the keenness of her observation, her irony and her playful wit."

For American composers, opera—except for *Porgy and Bess*—was relatively unimportant until the latter half of the twentieth century. After Menotti's post-Puccini period, our composers concentrated on topical American subjects and idioms. The last quarter of the century saw the rise of "CNN operas." A two-hundred-year-old British love story hardly seemed relevant to American composers and impresarios of that mindset. But I agree with Anna Quindlen: "Jane Austen wrote not of war and peace, but of men, money, and marriage, the battlefield for women of her day and, surely, of our own."

Many twentieth-century composers probably ignored *Pride and Prejudice* because of its period. Austen's novels are so rooted in their time and place, it is hard to imagine them being sung to atonal or dissonant tonal music. I did not consider this a problem. That is not to say that I have limited myself in this opera to the musical styles of the early nineteenth century (the novel was published in 1813). While I have imitated certain stylistic characteristics of the period, particularly in the dances, I was writing to engage a twenty-first-century opera audience, which is just another way of saying that I was trying to compose inventive and expressive music that I would like to hear if *I* were in the audience. While it does not have the sardonic wit of *Tartuffe*, Austen's humor is full of irony, and at times broad caricature (Mrs. Bennet, Mr. Collins, Lady Catherine de Bourgh). But her mockery is more good-natured than Molière's. Every great book or play made into an opera deserves a musical style that does not contradict the personality or character of the author.

As one would expect, the music of *Pride and Prejudice* is tonal and melodic, but because the characters and situations are multifarious, so is the music. Like the novel, the opera changes gradually from comedy to poignant drama. Act I is full of gaiety, humor, and flirtation. Act II is deeper in feeling, suspense, and the possibility of tragedy before things get sorted out. It is, in its own way, a "grand opera." It uses chorus and dancers and sometimes calls for a split stage—that is, there is occasionally action in both the house and the garden at the same time. The size of the orchestra, however, is moderate: somewhere between the instrumentation of *Figaro* and *Carmen*.

Despite those impresarios who are still looking only for works that are "challenging" and "cutting-edge," I believe that *Pride and Prejudice* will end up as my most popular opera. Even Stravinsky, the greatest innovator of the twentieth century, said in a lecture at Harvard, "I am beginning to think, in full agreement with the general public, that melody must keep its place at the summit of the hierarchy of elements that make up music." That sounds like an echo of the advice Verdi gave not long before he wrote his two greatest operas: "Let us turn back to the past; it will be a step forward."

✻ ✻ ✻

The years between finishing an opera and seeing it produced have been just as long and frustrating for *Pride and Prejudice* as for my other operas. But they did give me time to make two thoroughgoing revisions, including a new beginning and an expanded finale. I have also used the hiatus to write this book and to accept a number of choral commissions.

Rossini, after twenty years of seclusion, began composing again and called his new piano and chamber works "Sins of My Old Age." The half-dozen or so choral works I have written recently could be called "Songs of My Old Age"—all of them, one way or another, are about singing (several also involve laughing), and I either wrote the texts myself or translated, edited, adapted, or juxtaposed parts of public-domain texts. I can't judge their quality, of course, but each piece is unique. It seems that my experience with opera has changed my way of writing choral music. There is a curious progression here. As a young choral composer I gradually moved from setting texts verbatim to seeking larger forms by combining and adapting them into cycles, cantatas, and suites, until finally I decided it was time to write operas. And now that I am once again writing choral music, I can't stop acting like a librettist.

Blame Eliza Rubenstein. This group of choral pieces began with a commission for the fifteenth anniversary of her Orange County Women's Chorus. Eliza and I are old friends but we couldn't agree on a text. She wanted a poem that would celebrate achievement, an epitome of how far the chorus had come since its founding. Fine, but I didn't like the poems she suggested, and she found something wrong with everything I offered. In desperation, I wrote my own text called "We Can Sing That!" which showed her chorus's skill at singing all kinds of music in every sort of style: "beautiful melody . . . counterpoint . . . sad, glad . . . madrigals . . . harmony—we can sing anything!" The singers pulled it off *con brio,* and I made an SATB version for Robert Geary's Volti Chamber Chorus, which they premiered for their thirty-fifth anniversary.

Next in this group was "Daybreak in Alabama" (SSAA or SATB, a cappella) to a poem by Langston Hughes that begins, "When I get to be a composer. . . . " This felt to me like the beginning of a child's aria, and that's the way I set it; the choir sings the accompaniment. I have a special feeling for the works of Langston Hughes because we share Topeka as a place important to our upbringing, particularly the old public library that used to stand on the grounds of the state capitol. Hughes wrote that that was where he first developed a lifelong love for libraries and librarians. The same can be said of my father, and of me and my siblings. Hughes and I also share a connection to John Brown. The poet was proud that his maternal grandmother was first married to Lewis Sheridan Leary, who joined Brown's raid at Harpers Ferry and was killed there. "Daybreak" was commissioned by Robert Geary's Piedmont Choirs; I was happy to have the chance to add my music to this beautiful poem. Disguised as the simple dream of a child, it is a moving metaphor for Hughes's profound wish for justice and equality.

The next two "songs of my old age" were both premiered in the spring of 2014. "Laugh Till the Music Stops: Passacaglia and Canon" (SATB, piano) is an adaptation of part of a poem by John Masefield, commissioned by the Kirkland (WA) Choral Society, Dr. Glenn Gregg, conductor. "Green Music" (SSAA, a cappella) is based on various words by Hildegard von Bingen (1098–1179) that I translated and adapted, beginning with, "Through all eternity, green is the living spirit." It was commissioned by the Peninsula Women's Chorus, Dr. Martín Benvenuto, conductor, who had asked for something with an "eternity" theme. The choir sings a round on this theme, one that has no ending and that moves round and round through a circle of fifths.

I have completed but not yet heard three newer choral pieces: a short, a cappella introit, "Brothers and Sisters" (adapted from Hebrews 1–2), written for the Unitarian Universalist Church of San Francisco, Robert Sumner, conductor, and two ambitious works for chorus and piano. The first of these, "The Gift of Singing," is a seven-minute piece that I presented to the University of Kansas in gratitude for its honorary doctorate. I wrote the piece with the feeling that it was an autobiography. I chose a wide variety of texts, both poignant and humorous, beginning with a poem by George Dillon:

> I have no thing that is mine sure
> To give you, I am born so poor.
> Whatever I have was given me:
> The earth, the air, the sun, the sea.
> If I have anything to give
> Made surely of the life I live,
> It is a song that I have made.
> Now in your keeping it is laid.

(Poem by George Dillon [1906–1968]. Original title: "Serenader," first published in Poetry Magazine *28 [5], Chicago, 1926. Used by the kind*

permission of Helen Sussmann Parker, trustee of Dillon's literary estate.)

I marked the music *"Adagio semplice,* like a folk song." Later, following music from a traditional hymn, "How Can I Keep from Singing?" it touches in rapid succession on a wide variety of quotations, from: "The only thing better than singing is more singing" (Ella Fitzgerald) to "I don't sing because I'm happy; I'm happy because I sing" (William James).

Below is a bit of the text I put together for my second ambitious piece about singing, "Satan Hates Music," inspired by the writings of Martin Luther. It was commissioned by the Stockton (CA) Chorale, Magen Solomon, conductor, to be premiered the following season by the same chorale under its interim conductor, Daniel Hughes.

✿ ✿ ✿

> Satan hates music!
> It drives away the evil spirit.
> He loves trouble! He loves pain!
> Music consoles every grieving heart;
> It is the noblest of every art.
> Satan hates laughter!
> It makes him angry!
> So laugh at Satan!
> Sing joyful music;
> Laugh at Satan!
> Ha ha ha ha ha ha ha!

Did Martin Luther really write the words, "Satan hates music"? Yes, he did, as well as some of the other phrases in this piece. As translator and "librettist," I have taken many liberties and have added similar sentiments broadly inspired by the diverse writings of the great German theologian.

As for the music, what better model could a composer find than that greatest of all Lutherans, J. S. Bach? The piece is in a neo-Baroque style, and I have quoted two of Bach's best-known tunes—not the vocal lines, but the accompaniments. Most listeners will recognize the melodies I have taken from "Sheep May Safely Graze" (cantata 208) and "Sleepers Awake" (cantata 140). Their beautiful simplicity makes them a perfect foil for the children to sing in response to the devilish music of Satan. (The sopranos and altos of the adult choir sing these Bach tunes when the piece is performed without the optional children's chorus.) More than half a century ago, when I sang in the Stanford University Choir, these melodies haunted me. It has pleased me enormously to give them words in such an appropriate context. I also discovered that the first section of Bach's G-minor Fugue from Book 2 of *The Well-Tempered Clavier* (with a few tweaks to the vocal lines) perfectly fits the words, "Laugh at Satan!"

25

CODA

A Summing-Up

What can we conclude about the strange direction music took in the twentieth century? It was clearly a faster, more reckless journey than that recorded in any previous era. Countless composers veered off the path and left their audiences behind. Never before have so many composed so much for so few. The situation has improved somewhat in the new millennium, but the great gulf between composers and audiences will remain until we understand what happened to music in the last century. We must stop pretending that what happened was nothing more than the growing pains which new music has *always* encountered.

I have said that the western world has come to worship new gods: science and technology. How has this changed our way of thinking? Because science is by its nature a logical, cumulative discipline, new knowledge—and the application of it, which is technology—repeatedly supersedes the old. Cars replace buggies; computers replace typewriters. But should atonality replace tonality? Due to our altered mindset, some of us have erroneously applied scientific criteria to art, which, as I pointed out in the prelude, is essentially a means of communication: It is a language, not a science. We have allowed music to be treated as if it were just another specialized, constantly improving technology with its own "expert" caste to whom the nonprofessional is supposed to look for guidance. In the nineteenth century Mark Twain wrote, "I'm told that Wagner's music is better than it sounds." It was a joke then. But substitute "Stockhausen" for "Wagner," and some twentieth-century listeners said the same thing in deadly earnest.

It's easier to fool the public about music than about literature. Everyone can write words. Many write doggerel and are sure they could write a novel if they just had the time. But music is a mystery. Few people have any idea how to compose or even write down a simple tune. So we shouldn't be surprised that when Mr. Music Patron hears a new orchestral piece he doesn't understand, he blames himself rather than the composer. But he thinks nothing of dispatching a scathing letter to a Book-Review editor accusing Ms. Booker-Prize Winner of writing deplorable prose.

One of Arnold Schoenberg's fundamental beliefs was this: "If it is art, it is not for everybody, and if it is for everybody, it is not art." Well, of course that's true—if you mean by "everybody" *all* people, nonmusical as well as musical, illiterate as well as educated. I prefer the remark I heard years ago: "A masterpiece is still a masterpiece even if a million people say it is."

Schoenberg was a splendid musician; he deserves our sympathy for his suffering at the hands of the Nazis, who labeled his music "degenerate" (as they did all modern music) and drove him, a Jew, out of Europe. Only a man with such formidable intelligence and character could have garnered so much influence and have attracted such followers as Berg and Webern.

Schoenberg's theory of twelve-tone music—which proclaimed that each tone was equal and independent, and banished triadic harmony and all other vestiges of tonality—was claimed to be scientific and inevitable. By 1910 some music had indeed become densely chromatic, but it was absurd to consider atonality the inevitable result of this trend. (Bach wrote extremely chromatic pieces within the framework of tonality three hundred years ago.) A quick look at some composers who wrote tonal works of strikingly different kinds in the twentieth century shows how spurious these claims of inevitability were. In order of birthdate, the composers include Janáček, Debussy, Sibelius, Beach, Vaughan Williams, Ravel, de Falla, Bloch, Bartók, Stravinsky, Kodály, Prokofiev, Hindemith, Bacon, Thompson, Gershwin, Auric, Chávez, Poulenc, Copland, Rodrigo, Walton, Blitzstein, Shostakovich, Barber, Menotti, Britten, Bernstein, Nixon, Theodorakis, Floyd, Shchedrin, Pärt,

Glass, Corigliano, Lauridsen, Paulus, Adams, Larsen, Chen Yi, MacMillan, Kernis, Heggie, Torke, Puts, and Auerbach, among many others.

Indeed, the twentieth century gave us a great diversity of music; it is baffling how one "school" of composition could arrogate to itself so much authority. One can understand how the public could be fooled, but what drew so many academic composers to this mission?

The twelve-tone "system" is essentially intellectual and scientific. Perhaps these two adjectives help explain why academic composers were drawn to Schoenberg's music. After all, universities concern themselves chiefly with intellectual subjects—history, science, philosophy—and with research. So it is not surprising that this new "science" of music should come within the purview of institutions of higher learning.

The study of music at universities was rare in earlier times. Most nineteenth-century curricula offered very few music courses even for the general student, let alone a degree in music. But today, in many American schools of higher education, a student can graduate with a Bachelor of *Science* in music. The distinction between art and science has all but disappeared. And so has the difference between music conservatories and the large schools of music in many universities. Stanford University did not offer a major in music until 1946; now its music department is best known for its Center for Computer Research in Music and Acoustics.

* * *

When I first heard Schoenberg's *Pierrot Lunaire*, I was fascinated. Only a master could have written it. It was a 1912 "melodrama," chamber music written a decade before the composer had formulated his twelve-tone technique. It uses atonality and *Sprechstimme* (a cross between singing and speaking) to illustrate such poems as "Moondrunk," "The Sick Moon," "A Gallows Song," and eighteen others. It is a highly evocative musical picture of insanity. And there, in a nutshell, is the problem when atonality is used for more normal musical purposes.

The essence of atonality is disorder. It disrupts the musical language that has been "spoken" in the western world for centuries and still is. Atonality continues to sound confusing, chaotic, and lawless to most music lovers. That made it useful in a work like Berg's opera, *Wozzeck*, where the partial use of atonality to depict the derangement and alienation of its characters is effective. His second opera, *Lulu*, is not convincing to me, perhaps because incessant twelve-tone rows are utilized for characters who are not so deranged as those in his earlier opera.

Much more important for the history of music was Debussy—twelve years older than Schoenberg—whose genius opened up multiple new ways to reinvigorate the tonal language. In my opinion, the Mussorgsky-Debussy-Ravel-Stravinsky-Prokofiev-Gershwin thread was the more important, consequential transition from nineteenth- to twentieth-century music. To me, Schoenberg represents a cold, rigid winter of our musical language, Debussy a playful, colorful spring. In him can be seen both the past and the future of music. Almost every piece was like a new sprout from fertile ground. Comparing him to the Germans and Austrians of his time, I am tempted to call Debussy the savior of music.

Atonality is most problematic in opera, where music must portray human characters. Not only can a tonal opera convey vivid aural representations of character and personality, but also it can even subtly contradict the words a character is singing. Consider Iago's poisonous lies to Otello: they are delivered in music of great sincerity, but Verdi overdoes it just enough to make us shudder. I tried something similar, but comic, with the hypocrite Tartuffe—he mouths deep religious piety, but the audience can tell from his fake Gregorian chant that he's a phony.

Many of us have had the excruciating experience of witnessing atonal operas that attempt to portray normal people in normal situations. From the music, however, you can't tell a love scene from a nervous breakdown. I have also heard resolutely tonal operas suddenly switch into atonality because one of the characters is confused or troubled. I find this tactic ineffective, mainly because it applies a sledgehammer where nuance is needed. It unnerves the audience, as would the characters in a play if they suddenly began speaking a private language.

A hundred years ago, atonality was defended as a new language to which we would soon become accustomed. Schoenberg said that musical people would hear *Pierrot Lunaire* and "go away whistling the tunes." Of his twelve-tone system, he wrote a friend, "I have made a discovery which will ensure the supremacy of German music for the next hundred years." Richard Strauss's opinion was, "The only person who can help poor Schoenberg now is a psychiatrist." Ravel said, "That isn't music—it's lab work." Indeed, Schoenberg claimed that his twelve-tone system was equivalent to Albert Einstein's theory of relativity. Once again we find this fallacious analogy between art and science.

Please think back now to the scientist's words that I quoted in the prelude. Stephen Jay Gould attributed the inaccessibility of new music to the misplaced value we ascribe to innovation, to "this perpetual striving toward novelty." John Adams, in his memoir, *Hallelujah Junction*, takes issue with Gould. He says that Gould draws the wrong conclusion. "This is the fondly imagined hope of the musical amateur," Adams writes, "the listener who wishes the present state of confusion in the arts would just go away." But I don't think we composers should dismiss as "amateurs" those listeners who disagree with us. The root of the word "amateur" is "love," as in "music lovers"—the very people we compose for. "Surprising as it may appear for someone as independent as Brahms," writes Jan Swafford in his biography of that composer, "he considered the verdict of the middle-class public to be the ultimate arbiter. . . . The final court of any musician was the ears, hearts, and minds of listeners."

But it was unnecessary for a fine composer like Adams to cross swords with Gould at all. John Adams is one of the most popular of living composers. In fact, he figured prominently in the minimalist movement that struck the first organized blow against the atonal fortress: dedicated simplicity against relentless complexity.

What is most important is that some of these minimalist composers soon extended their scope, and have written a new, refreshing kind of tonal music. It may sometimes lack melody and variety, but it has produced some entertaining and inventive music that has attracted audiences and is still developing. Furthermore, it inspired many composers of the next generation. (I do not name them because I would have to leave out more than I could include.) But I am not claiming that tonal music is any guarantee of excellence. As in every art in every period, only a fraction of what is produced has lasting, universal value. As long ago as the 1780s, young Beethoven's mentor, Christian Neefe, urged composers to attain "an understanding of the whole substance of music," so that it would become "no empty cling-clang, no sounding brass or tinkling cymbal." (See Jan Swafford's *Beethoven: Anguish and Triumph*.) The value of that advice became painfully clear recently when I heard a young composer's brilliantly orchestrated work for huge orchestra that perfectly matched Neefe's "empty-cling-clang" description.

"Sounding brass and tinkling cymbal" is from 1 Corinthians 13:1–2, and was used by Brahms in his last work, *Vier ernste Gesänge*: "Though I speak with the tongues of men and of angels and have not love [*agape*], I am become as sounding brass and tinkling cymbal."

This is not the first time in music history that synthesis has become more important than expansion. The early classicists, reacting against the polyphonic excesses of the late Baroque, produced music that aimed for more clarity and balance. And some individual composers in every period—Brahms is a good example—have been more interested in deepening and developing than in forging new paths.

Some of the minimalists not only reacted against atonal music, but also joined my generation of tonal composers in rejecting the nihilists of mid-century, who had retreated into bizarre experiments in Dada and random sounds, believing that they were reinvigorating music. Schoenberg told John Cage that Cage was an inventor, not a composer. (I think he was just being kind.) But great composers—even those who have been called revolutionaries—have always "spoken" the same basic language as their audiences have. Their tone, accent, and what they are saying may have been new, but forget the myth that Mozart and Beethoven were not understood in their own day.

Certain unloved twentieth-century composers—and writers who wanted to curry their favor—greatly distorted the historical record. Yes, there is a *Lexicon of Musical Invective* that purports to prove that all great music was unappreciated in its own day. But an even larger lexicon could be compiled of the praise, gratitude, and love that the great composers of the past received, and still do. Why else would tens of thousands of people have lined the streets of Vienna for Beethoven's funeral procession? To fall back on the cliché that "new music has always been rejected by audiences" is not only historically incorrect, but also misleading. It attempts to conceal the breach between tonal and atonal music—a chasm so deep that nothing like it had ever been seen before.

The chaotic state of new music in the twentieth century caused some listeners to reject *all* contemporary works. They stopped listening at the first hint of a dissonance or melodic shape foreign to the nineteenth century. For new music, they preferred the blandest, dullest imitations of what they already knew. Here's an example.

After a performance of my opera *Tartuffe* some years ago, the audience was invited to ask questions. An elderly gentleman in the front row immediately rose from his seat and addressed a question to me: "Why don't you composers write melodies anymore?" The singers and directors came to my defense; one sang the beginning of the opera's most popular aria, "Fair Robin I Love," but my inquisitor was not appeased. It was only later that I realized what he was *really* asking: "Why don't you write melodies that we already know, as Verdi and Puccini did?" (As if "Va Pensiero" and "Nessun Dorma" were already famous when their operas were premiered.)

* * *

If you did not live through the post-war era, you may think I am exaggerating the importance accorded to atonality in the latter half of the twentieth century. I suggest you take a look at almost any history of that century's music. You will probably find that the second half of the book is a recital of the trends, –isms, novelties, systems, movements, experiments, fads, and lunacies of the period, nearly all of which were attempts to escape from tonality. These are treated not as detours or dead ends, but as important developments. Rarely do these authors connect them to the decline of public interest in new classical music. When the more evolutionary composers are mentioned—Walton, Gershwin, Kodaly, or Barber—it is with an insinuation that they were not important. The authors of such books and articles mean no harm; they were simply taught, like almost everyone else, that only the "innovators," the "mavericks," were significant. Such authors hardly ever discuss contemporary composers in the larger context of their lasting value to music lovers—indeed, to humanity. Imagine a history of late *nineteenth*-century music that devoted most of its attention to Liszt, Bruckner, and Hugo Wolf, but little to those notorious reactionaries Brahms, Tchaikovsky, and Dvorak. (Wolf is reported to have said, "One single cymbal crash by Bruckner is worth all four symphonies of Brahms.")

* * *

What's wrong with atonality? What makes it sound insane? To understand what is meant by *atonality*, you need to know what *tonality* is, and what a vast, complex musical language it implies. If you are a musician, please be patient while I give a simplified explanation for less-learned readers. I have never seen an adequate exploration of this subject, which is essential to understanding what happened to classical music.

Nearly all western music (folk, popular, and classical) has for centuries been in one or another *key*, or *tonality*. Imagine a very simple song in the key of C. That means the note C is the home base, the starting and ending point of a scale: C, D, E, F, G, A, B, C. Neither the melody nor the chords in the accompaniment use any other notes but those— no E-flats, no G-sharps, nor any other "chromatic" tones. If you play the song on the piano you will use only the white keys.

The basic chords are called triads because each is made up of three notes. The "home" triad in the key of C consists of C, E, and G (skipping one note of the scale between each member of the triad.) Triads may be formed starting on any note of the scale. All but one are called consonant, because they sound satisfying to our ears. They relate to a harmonic series found in nature. When other notes are added to the triad, they produce what was traditionally called dissonance, which had to be resolved into consonance if the ear was to be satisfied.

Over the centuries this very basic scheme evolved into the magnificent system of tonality used variously from Bach to Brahms to Bartok (as in his *Concerto for Orchestra*) and to the present day, even though it may encompass many new kinds of melodies, chords, chromatic notes, and dissonances. This is our inherited language; it makes possible a rich emotional and intellectual world. By setting up conflicts—between consonance and dissonance, for instance—composers can take the listener on a melodic and dramatic journey of expectations, suspense, surprise, deception, and satisfaction—not to mention the landscape along the way: beautiful and powerful harmonies, counter-melodies, and tonal textures. These are not possible in a musical world in which *everything* is dissonant.

Modulation from one key to another—a basic way to get variety—is obviously impossible if there are no keys. So are modal changes between major, minor, and the older modes. In chapter 4 I mentioned the magical interplay between traditional harmony and counterpoint; that interplay is missing where there is no tonal harmony. Likewise, in atonality we miss the ever-present harmonic changes of tonal music that are so fascinating in their variety and rate of change, so compelling in their ability to give a sense of forward movement or repose, and, above all, so satisfying in their foundation of consonance.

Moreover, the interaction between the expected and the unexpected makes possible incongruous relationships—the source of most humor. Nothing falls so flat as an atonal scherzo. If everything is incongruous, nothing is incongruous. In my opinion, atonal music has only the *gestures* of traditional music, but not the language. If you have ever attended a play in a language you didn't understand, you know what I mean. Without a common language, there can be no satire, no irony, nor any of the other artful nuances that enrich music.

Yet none of these characteristics of atonality are so fatal to music as the absence of memorable melody. Theoretically, an atonal melody can be sung and remembered; in practice that is rarely possible. To be able to remember what you have heard is crucial to following musical development. How can you enjoy such elemental musical pleasures as variation and recapitulation if you can't even recognize what has come before, to say nothing of the fundamental pleasure of beautiful, distinctive, and singable melody?

                         ❊ ❊ ❊

All this has been a way of explaining why atonal music sounds to me—and possibly to you—gray and arbitrary. I hope this explanation will console those who have repeatedly and unsuccessfully tried to like music that others claim to be "progressive." Be assured that most professional musicians don't like atonal music either. But please note: not all unconventional music is atonal. There have been and still are inventive composers who tweak tonality in unusual and fascinating ways, with or without electronic sounds. Think of many of the works of Olivier Messiaen, for example. Still, you the listeners are the final judges of whether a new piece lives or dies. This should not be construed as a responsibility, or even an opportunity; it's simply the consequence of believing your own ears.

I'm sure that my colleagues who compose or perform atonal music will dispute much of what I have written, and they are welcome to do so. I repeat that my opinions are based upon my experience as a listener, as a human being. Atonal music has always left me cold, but there were many twentieth-century composers I loved before I ever studied music. When I first heard Bartok's brand-new *Concerto for Orchestra* in 1947, I felt that a fabulous world had been opened up to me. It truly was a life-changing experience. The first time I heard Stravinsky's *Petrushka* and Prokofiev's *Romeo and Juliet,* I felt much the same way.

And I am happy to hear any new piece that delights, moves, or fascinates me.

But in my old age I don't worry about any of this. I have followed my bliss and my own taste all my life, and I expect other musicians and music lovers to do the same. What sounds ugly to me may be an inspiration to someone else. The advice I give to young composers is simply a quotation from Oscar Wilde: "Be yourself; everyone else is already taken."

I have chosen to compose in the language I inherited—shaping and changing it according to my own ideas and personality, as a novelist or playwright does. I can't imagine wanting to divorce myself completely from that virtuoso and still flexible language that has been built up for centuries by countless composers.

Great art is more than beautiful, more than joyful, more than exciting, more than consoling. It is life-affirming. It brings forth our greatest faith in the human race. When I hear overwhelmingly magnificent music, I feel wonder and gratitude that one human being has been able to construct such splendor. Tears come to my eyes, as they do when I walk into an exhibit and am suddenly struck by the immense beauty of a painting. If human beings can conceive of such visions and achieve the profound skill to make them live in the hearts of all of us, what are we not capable of? A work of art is a celebration of our humanity—not only the humanity of its creator and re-creators, but also the capacity of *all* humans to understand, to love, and to be nourished by art. This phenomenon is a kind of miracle that we must forever treasure.

APPENDIX A

The Text Trap

From the Choral Journal, *November 2005*
Reprinted in Composers on Composing for Choir, *Tom Wine, ed.,*
GIA, 2007

At the heart of choral music is a paradox. A choral piece shapes and is shaped by its text, but because audiences rarely understand the words, they usually hear and judge the piece as pure music.

This paradox creates a double trap for composers. If we obsess on the text, squeezing disparate musical imagery and emotion out of every line, the listener may hear only disjointed musical episodes. If we pay little attention to the text, focusing on the creation of a satisfying musical form, the result may be a disappointing disconnect between words and music.

Today's composers are more liable to fall into the first trap—obsessing on the text. I hear too many new choral pieces that lack musical organization. I'll return to this shortly with some advice on avoiding the text trap, but first let's consider some historical reasons for the modern ascendancy of words over music.

Choral texts today—in this article I am referring chiefly to shorter works—are often secular poems intended to be sung by secular choruses for concert audiences. In the "golden age" of choral music, the texts were more often sacred, sung by church choirs for church congregations. (English and Italian madrigals of the period were written for private singing, not for audiences.) What are the musical implications of the differences between sacred and secular texts?

Secular poems are more varied and less universally known than most sacred texts. They may be about practically anything: love, nature, humor, death, morality, music—you name it. This lively variety invites more attention to the text than does one more "Gloria," "Kyrie" or psalm setting; the congregation already knows most of those texts. Another obvious reason that the text has become more important today is that secular poems are usually sung by and for people who speak the language of the poem. Concert goers are in general more curious participants than Sunday worshipers; they have paid for a ticket and expect to understand what's going on. (Another paradox: we *know* they won't get all the words, but we still expect them to.)

To be sure, choral composers are still writing sacred music. The results are excellent when gifted composers write new and beautiful settings of well known texts; they concentrate on the music just because the texts *are* so well known. The results are *not* so excellent when composers repeat the formulas of older periods, or set mawkish new texts to mawkish music. I find it interesting that in the serious choral field, many of the most popular pieces written in my lifetime have been those with well-known sacred texts, e.g. *Alleluia* (Thompson), *O Magnum Mysterium* (Lauridsen), *Ave Maria* (Biebl). These are touching works, not because of their text settings, but because their music is beautiful and skillfully constructed. Remember: Bach and Handel sometimes paid little heed to words; they used the same glorious music for different texts.

These sacred pieces show one way to avoid domination by the text. But they do not interest me as much as today's secular choral music, which I believe offers more of an opportunity precisely *because* secular poetry is varied, full of character, and modern in its sensibilities, whether spiritual or worldly. But how often, after hearing a new setting, have we come away with the impression that the composer simply set the poem one line after another with no over-all musical plan? This is not composition; this is a catalog of musical ideas: six melodies in search of a composition.

It is not beside the point to observe here that new operas have the same problem. It often seems that the producer, the director and the librettist have bullied the composer into abdicating his/her age-old right to be in charge—to compose an opera with dramatic musical forms. Here, too, we often end up with a parade of ideas without any substantial musical satisfaction. Great operas have been written to mediocre texts; none have been written with fragmentary music, no matter how good the libretto. Likewise, no choral piece remains in the repertory because of its words.

We choral composers must also exercise dramatic control over our texts. We must not allow them to bully us into slavish obedience. True, some short poems are so perfectly constructed that the choral composer should simply set them "as is," perhaps as simple homophonic songs. Even so, the music will not sound as perfect as the poem unless the composer's skill in creating a cohesive, integrated work is as great as the poet's.

Recently I decided to put to a test my belief in the primacy of music in choral composition. I wrote a *Suite for Chorus*, subtitled *Songs Without Words,* four pieces that use wordless vowels and consonants in somewhat the same way string music uses various bow strokes and pizzicato (not a new idea). While I took great pains to compose the work specifically for choral singers, I had no text to fall back on for emotional content or formal organization. I had only the devices that composers of instrumental music have—which are considerable: melodic and motivic invention, development, repetition, variation, suspense, climax, contrast, unity, variety—and tried to create a satisfying musical journey. For younger composers, and also for experienced choral composers who may suspect that words have been bullying their music, I heartily recommend this kind of wordless discipline. But please don't misunderstand me. I am not advocating that you try to pour your text into a conventional musical form such as sonata, rondo, or ABA. Though I could give you successful examples of all of these, I could also give you disastrous examples.

[I later put words to the *Suite for Chorus* mentioned above, being careful to retain the characteristic sounds of the originals. The individual pieces became: (1) Spiritual, "Kum Ba Yah"; (2) Folksong Madrigal, "Too Young to Marry"; (3) Requiem, "They That Mourn"; (4) Fairy Tale, "Papageno and the Prince." I am indebted to two conductors and their singers—Dr. Hilary Apfelstadt with the Ohio State University Chorale and Dr. James Kim with the Colorado State University Chamber Choir—for trying out these works in manuscript; and also to Clara Longstreth with the New Amsterdam Singers, who earned a glowing review from the *Times* for their New York premiere of the published work, June 4, 2010.]

✦ ✦ ✦

Please allow me now to try to help the young choral composer avoid the text trap. My first published choral pieces were written more than a half-century ago; I have learned from my own mistakes and from the successes and mistakes of others. But I cannot presume to tell anyone how to write a good choral piece. This is how *not* to write one. Good composers—and there are many of them today—can write fine pieces in countless ways, including, I'm sure, by ignoring what I am saying. I am only passing on what I have learned.

If I have spoken of a "text trap," don't think for a minute that I believe the text is unimportant. That is where the choral composer begins, and where the choral conductor and singer *ought* to begin. But to write choral works with musical integrity, our first task is to understand the several kinds of structure in the poem we are going to set, especially the inner, psychological structure on which we will build our musical form. Since the wrong poem may doom us right from the start, our real first task is to *choose* the poem. I sometimes look at several hundred before finding the right one. Whenever I find a promising poem I put it into a file, where later it may turn out to be just what I want. (E. A. Robinson's poem, "Richard Cory," had been in my file forty years before I found an appropriate place for it in the cycle, *An American Trio*.)

How do you tell a good poem for choral music from a bad one? First, you have to love it. Poems and music live in the emotions. If you feel no emotion for a poem, neither will your singers or listeners. But not all poems you love will make good choral pieces. Difficult philosophical poems are not good candidates. Choosing poetry is highly subjective, but I'll venture a few observations, keeping in mind that we are looking for texts that invite musical translation. (It truly is translation; the poem is being transferred from one language to another. Good translators respect the idiomatic and structural differences between languages.)

(1) I like direct, simple diction. Singing is an elemental experience. How much stronger, simpler and more natural is the word "stop" than its more learned synonyms, "terminate," "cease," "discontinue." The

poetry of the King James Bible, with its short Anglo-Saxon words that we have spoken all our lives, is much more natural and satisfying to sing than are revised, accurate, scientific versions. I even stay away from great poems whose language is obscure for any reason. If you have trouble understanding a poem when reading it, think how impossible it will become when sung by forty people or submerged in choral counterpoint. Complex ideas severely limit musical development because they are already dense. (Complex and profound are not the same thing; a poem or a piece of music may be profound but simple.)

(2) Short poems give a composer the most latitude for musical metamorphosis. Look at *The Messiah:* Handel broke up the long text into very short segments. "And with His stripes we are healed" is a five-page piece built on just seven words. Thompson's *Alleluia:* one word. But I see composers today choosing texts a page long for a three-minute choral piece. Has a law been passed against repeating words? Or do these composers believe that if the text is printed in the program, the audience won't notice the absence of musical continuity? (Some opera composers nowadays make the same mistake in relying on super-titles to keep the audience interested. Titles are helpful for older operas in foreign languages—those operas had musical integrity to start with— but super-titles do not supply *musical* drama where there is none.)

(3) The poetic quality—imagery—naturally attracts composers. This, however, is obvious; I don't think many composers are apt to choose poems that don't "sound" musical. There may be such a thing, however, as too much imagery. I have rejected poems that had so many references to sounds, instruments, noises that I was afraid music would be redundant. This kind of text sorely tempts the composer just to chase the words around. There are brilliant exceptions, but these texts don't often appeal to me. The only poem of this kind I have ever set was suggested by the commissioning chorus: "Pied Beauty" by Gerard Manley Hopkins. I was against it, but careful study gradually engendered enthusiasm and stretched my horizon. I was well aware, however, that with such a text, I would have to be particularly careful to provide a musical structure to support all the jingling and jangling, so the piece turned out pretty well. It is the finale of my cycle, *The Children of David: Five Modern Psalms.* I chose to use a recurring long line as a kind of ritornello, a scaffold on which to hang the bursts of color.

(4) Poetic diction is related to imagery, but is different. It is defini-
tive in the poem and should be honored in the musical setting. Fine
lyric poets are masters of poetic diction. What composer could resist the
inherent music in "Let It Be Forgotten," by Sara Teasdale (1884-1933),
which I used in the cycle, *The Winds of May:*

> Let it be forgotten as a flower is forgotten,
> Forgotten as a fire that once was singing gold.
> Let it be forgotten for ever and ever
> Time is a kind friend, he will make us old.
>
> If anyone asks, say it was forgotten,
> Long and long ago,
> As a flower, as a fire, as a hushed foot-fall
> In a long forgotten snow.

(Poem from Flame and Shadow, *first published 1920 by Henry Holt Co.*
The Winds of May *re-published 2003 by G. Schirmer, Inc., New York)*

Because of the poem's simplicity and repetitions, a composer can build
polyphonic music upon it without threatening the listener's comprehension, and without obscuring the quiet but heartbreaking emotion of the
poem.

I learned a good lesson about poetic diction from my father, a fine
poet, many of whose poems I have set. When I was considering "Pied
Beauty," he pointed out how effectively Hopkins had alternated short,
fast sounds with long, slow ones, particularly in the line "Whatever is
fickle, freckled (who knows how?)." Most of the poem glories in the
quick sounds of "dappled things," making the sudden long sounds all
the more effective. The composer must be aware of this kind of music
within a poem and make the most of it.

(5) Musical structure. Here we return to what I believe is the heart
of the matter. I said earlier that to write choral works with musical
integrity, our first task is to understand the several kinds of structure in
the poem we are going to set. Structure in poetry can include the
pattern of lines, meter, rhythm, or stanzas (couplets, tercets, quatrains)
or the larger fixed forms, such as the sonnet, ballad, limerick, sestina,
etc. You will also find invented forms, variations of fixed forms, and free
verse. We must recognize these forms when we set them, but our musical form will best be determined by another kind of structure—what I

have called the psychological or dramatic structure of a poem. (I mentioned that repetitive stanzas may sometimes require music that sticks close to the poetic structure, but this need not be a restriction; good composers can conjure countless variations on simple ideas.) To find this dramatic structure, we need to analyze the poem, observing the location of climaxes, of repose, of suspense, tension, changes of mood, returns to previous allusions or moods (with or without the same words.)

As an example, look back at Teasdale's poem, "Let It Be Forgotten." Study it as if you were going to set it for chorus. Take note of all the elements mentioned above and anything else that strikes you as a clue for your composition. After you have done this, go on to the following observations I am offering about the poem's possibilities for music.

The poem, it seems to me, is permeated with sadness, resignation, acceptance, and above all, a sense of the passing of time: "forgotten," "for ever and ever," "time...will make us old," "long and long ago," "long forgotten snow"—these are all of a piece. The first four words, "Let it be forgotten," form the motif of the poem. To an unusual degree, this motif suffuses the entire work. This suggests the use of some *musical* motif—one with the potential for variation. I would also consider the use of one of the old modes to convey and heighten the sense of a bygone time. (I used the Phrygian mode.)

The first three lines of the poem belong together; they are enlargements of the motif. Beginning with the second half of the first line, "as a flower is forgotten," this section seems to call for lyrical expression because of the alliteration, the flowing vowels, and particularly the phrase, "singing gold." Modulation might direct the flowing movement toward a new musical goal. An imitative texture could be derived from the motif, giving the composer an opportunity for a gentle rise and fall in the vocal range and dynamics.

The fourth line, however, is very different in its diction. The flowing movement stops. Read it aloud and you will see that its sounds are longer. "Time is a kind friend, he will make us old." This does, indeed, require more time, and demands a new musical treatment. It is a chance for variety, but you do not have to give up unity. You can change the texture, but retain some important element of the first section—a rhythmic pattern, for instance, or continue the atmosphere of your old modality. This fourth line is also a summing-up of the first stanza; it suggests a full cadence—most definitely not a half cadence—but not in the home key.

Is there anything remarkable about the first line of the second stanza, "If anyone asks"? This strikes me as the only time the author steps outside her omniscient point of view and becomes personal for a brief, but revealing moment. One voice part could sing this line alone. But the final words of the line, "say it was forgotten," lead back to the motivic idea, but are not quite the same. This is a chance to return to the lyrical melody, perhaps with imitation, but varied. The elongation of the words "long and long ago," echoing the "ah" sound in "forgotten," is made to order for singers. It is also made to order for composers who are trying to unify their piece in the same way the poet has unified hers. It doesn't take a genius to see that these words can be set to the motif in long notes as counterpoint to the lyrical lines.

For the ending of the poem you have surely noticed that the poet brings back the flower and fire images, extending the "f" alliteration with "a hushed foot-fall." The last line of the poem, "In a long forgotten snow," returns to the key word of the motif, "forgotten." I have often said that Sara Teasdale must have loved music, because she made her poems so easy for composers to set. Here she has given us the opportunity for recapitulation of several melodic elements from the first stanza, as well as the golden chance to end our piece with the same motif that began it.

Unfortunately, not many poems are so composer-friendly. And I hasten to add that my analysis is by no means the only one possible. Every poem is open to different interpretations. I would guess, moreover, that most experienced composers make this kind of analysis intuitively. (Writing this down was harder than composing the music).

But whether the poem we choose is composer-friendly or not, the important thing is that we remain true to its psychological/dramatic form, rather than to its outer structure. No two sonnets share exactly the same dramatic structure any more than do any two sonatas. By discovering the structure that lies *within* the poem, you will be well on your way to finding the right musical structure. Only when that becomes clear should the composer begin to write music. The music itself will alter, modify and enrich your original concept, but rarely should you let it beguile you into giving up your concept entirely.

This seems like a good place to leave young composers—at work writing music with a good idea of the shape their work will take. They surely know, however, that their choral piece will not be judged by its *shape*, which will be as invisible to most listeners as is the steel infrastructure that holds up the concert hall. Nor will it be judged by its text. The piece will be judged by the beauty and the character and the individuality of its melodies and harmonies, and by the skill of the poem's translation to the choral medium. We wouldn't be composers if we did not happily accept that challenge. I hope that my suggestions may help my younger colleagues look at a poem as the framework for an imaginative musical form, not as a straitjacket. Choral composition should not be the musical equivalent of painting by numbers.

APPENDIX B

Afterword from the Libretto to the Opera *John Brown*

It takes an epoch, it takes the whole of a society, it takes a national and religious birthpang to produce either Joan of Arc or John Brown. Everyone living at the time takes some part in the episode; and thereafter, the story remains as a symbol, an epitome of the national and religious idea which was born through the crisis. . . . John Brown is as big as a myth, and the story of him is an immortal legend—perhaps the only one in our history. —John Jay Chapman (1862–1933)

The legend of John Brown has often obscured the man behind it. For fifty years after Harpers Ferry there was hardly a writer who did not feel it necessary to take sides: either Brown was a martyred saint or a murdering madman. Although we now have well researched biographies that attempt to understand both man and myth, the controversy persists with surprising tenacity. One still encounters new books which, by wrenching Brown out of the context of his own time, attempt to prove some contemporary thesis.

The doctrinaire authors are not the only problem; many standard histories of the United States and of the Civil War perpetuate the old myths. For one thing, it is easier; for another, modern historians also have what Oliver Wendell Holmes called their "inarticulate major premises," which influence evaluations as much as do the facts.

What has all this to do with an *opera* about John Brown? Don't most people still believe with Dr. Johnson that opera is simply an exotic and irrational entertainment? I prefer to believe that in its fusion of drama and music, opera is the ideally extravagant medium to present the action and passion of the national struggle over slavery as epitomized in the larger-than-life figure of John Brown. Immortal legend, moral crisis, myth—these have always been the stuff of opera. (For Verdi and Wagner, the glory of opera was not only its musical power to stir the passions, but also its power to dramatize great ideas.) But as the tenacity of the John Brown controversy proves, the subject is still so topical, it has so many modern parallels, that even writers of opera must treat the man and the events with a sense of responsibility. We must seek to tell the important truths with as much honesty as historians, and must commit ourselves just as steadfastly to a selection of material which articulates not only our own "major premises," but competing ones as well. Fortunately, as all good historians and playwrights know, such conflict is the life blood of both history and drama.

The peculiar problem that historical dramatists face is this: which minor lies can they tell in order to dramatize the major truths? They must telescope some persons, places and events in order to put the story on stage. The writer of an historical *opera* must add to this the problem of arranging that the dramatic effect will be heightened by music, not burdened by it, as often happens in modern operas.

I suppose that only a fool would base his knowledge of history upon what he sees in the theater. And yet, from the time of the ancient Greeks, through Shakespeare's day to our own, so many people have done just that, that it makes me nervous about the opera's minor infidelities. (They are nothing, of course, compared to the racist distortions of *Santa Fe Trail*, an old Errol Flynn movie about Jeb Stuart and John Brown which still appears on television with depressing regularity.) Even though I can recommend several books to set the record straight, I know that most opera goers will not consult them. Therefore, in order to ease my conscience, defuse my critics and enlighten the public, I will point out the principal liberties I have taken.

First, let me repeat that my intention has been to tell the truth in all important respects. The personality of John Brown, for instance, I have tried to show in all its colors and contradictions: he was both tender and stern, passionate and reasonable, stubborn, shrewd, idealistic and practical. The important historical events in the opera did actually take place essentially as they are shown. It is with the lesser events and characters that I have taken the most liberties.

To begin with the first scene, Martha was not Tom Barber's sister; her name was Brewster, not Barber. Both she and Oliver were several years younger than I have shown them, and Tom was killed a day earlier. Lt. J. E. B. Stuart (later to become a Confederate Cavalry General) was in Kansas and did encounter John Brown there, but there is no evidence that he or his slave were at Lawrence December 8. I have attributed to him beliefs and personality traits of various Southern leaders, making him more representative of his class than he really was. Although he did come from a proud old Virginia slaveholding family, the real man was less political than I have shown him to be.

John Brown had six sons in Kansas; I have combined them into two, and added about ten years to his daughter Annie's age so that she could be present not only in the Maryland farm house (where she really was), but also in Kansas (where she was not). Frederick Douglass was an old friend of Brown and his family; the conversation they have about Brown's Allegheny plan was held in 1847 in Massachusetts, not in 1856 in Kansas, which Douglass never visited. The beating I show him receiving is an amalgam of several events, all actually occurring, but at other times and places: Douglass was beaten in several Northern states for making speeches against slavery; some of Brown's Pottawatomie neighbors were brutal men who had employed bloodhounds to catch runaway slaves; United States troops really were used to help uphold the bogus laws. The book burning did take place, but several days *after* the Pottawatomie executions.

The most serious hazard of showing Douglass beaten in this scene is the possible inference that it motivated Brown to instigate the Pottawatomie attack. I have taken great pains to show throughout the opera that Brown's reasons were quite otherwise, but I must admit the risk of misinterpretation is still there. I decided that the dramatic necessity of showing the sympathetic, brilliant black leader beaten by vicious slave runners—protected by United States troops—overrode the small risk. The basic truth seemed more important than the untruth of time and place. (Most of the words of Douglass's speech in this scene are his own, but I have compressed and edited them from his speeches and writings spanning many years.)

The meeting between Brown and Douglass before the Harpers Ferry raid took place two months earlier and some miles distant from Brown's hideout, but its outcome was the same. Shields Green and another escaped slave in Brown's troop, Dangerfield Newby, have been combined; the letters of Newby's wife have been condensed. Martha and Annie did keep house for the raiders; Martha was by this time married and pregnant, and there is some evidence that she moved from pacifism to abolitionism through her contact with the Brown family. Her parents opposed her marrying a "fanatical Brown," but most of the Oliver-Martha story had to be invented. My expectation is that many people will initially identify with Martha and see events through her eyes, learning with her, I hope, that peace cannot come before justice.

The Harpers Ferry scene telescopes events that took place from the second day of the raid, October 17, until the day of Brown's hanging, December 2. Brown was interrogated after the battle by Governor Wise, Lt. Stuart, other dignitaries and reporters, but not until hours later. The greatest liberty I have taken in this scene is in the swiftness of national events, not so much in the South—which went into panic immediately—but in the North, where reaction to the raid was at first almost uniformly negative. Thoreau was among the first to speak out in favor of Brown; it took some time for Northern shock to turn to sympathy for John Brown's courage, his unshakeable convictions and stirring words, but the majority never did approve of Harpers Ferry. Yet by the time he was hanged, his speech at trial and publication of his many letters had made Brown a hero to a vociferous, influential group of people all over the world. Victor Hugo declared: "The American Union must be considered dissolved. Between the North and South stands the gallows of Brown . . . for there is something more terrible than Cain slaying Abel—it is Washington slaying Spartacus."

In the Apotheosis I had once again to rearrange timetables for Martha and Frederick Douglass. Her baby had not yet been born, and by December 2, Douglass was no longer in the country and could not take part in any of the meetings which were held in churches and halls all over the North. But he had already spoken out for John Brown, and throughout his life continued to be one of the most eloquent defenders of the man he said "will need no defender . . . until the lives of tyrants and murderers shall become more precious in the sight of men than justice and liberty."

I hope that that time has not come, but a book published as recently as 1979 about Brown's supporters, *The Secret Six*, makes one wonder. Its author, Otto Scott—a writer of corporate histories—chooses to ignore the entrenchment of slavery, and argues (largely on the basis of long discredited sources) that Brown was the evil father of modern terrorism. Here we see why the controversy persists: the author's "inarticulate major premise"—that even tyrannical laws maintained by terror must never be opposed by force—distorts the meaning of the most important movement in the history of our country. Need I say that the major premise behind my opera is that the abolition of slavery was the foremost issue in nineteenth-century America and John Brown its most representative man? As Theodore Roosevelt wrote, "he embodied the inspiration of the men of his generation."

Was John Brown a terrorist? Terrorists kill innocent civilians massively and randomly. The five men executed by Brown's followers at Pottawatomie were carefully selected. They were participants in the pro-slavery terror in Kansas which had already resulted in the murder of six free-state men and in the sacking of Lawrence; they had publicly declared war on the Browns and other abolitionists. The killing at Pottawatomie was a terrible deed, but a just reprisal in Brown's biblical view. And from a historical perspective, we may ask whether Americans have not always supported fighting back against terror and oppression. It always amazes me to hear John Brown's raid at Harpers Ferry denounced by the same Americans who glorify the colonial farmers who killed British soldiers on their way back from Concord. As if "taxation without representation" was in any way commensurate with slavery, "one hour of which," in Jefferson's words, "is fraught with more misery than ages of that which [the colonials] rose in rebellion to oppose."

It is easy to think that whatever happened had to happen, but of course this is not so. If the outcome in Kansas had been different, or if there had been no John Brown, Frederick Douglass or Abraham Lincoln, the United States today could be a very different place. Civil war was probably inevitable, but had it been delayed until the South had acquired the vast new territories and resources it coveted, who knows what the result would have been?

But there will always be those who do not want to hear about a man so bent upon disturbing a long accepted order. The more comfortable we are, the less we want to be disturbed. Even Theodore Roosevelt added to his praise of Brown the warning—ironic, coming from him—that violence was no way to settle anything.

Here, then, is the nub of the question: if so many of mankind's heroes are those who sacrifice their lives in fighting tyranny, how can we deny the validity of all violence? It obviously depends on circumstances; these will differ in each case, so there will never be a final answer to this profound problem. Works of art have never been expected to solve problems; I believe that the best we can do is to show not only the "hero" as he really was, but the circumstances as well. Without that, no wisdom is possible.

In this regard, my long path to John Brown may be of interest. My father, Kirke Field Mechem, was head of the Kansas State Historical Society, and a writer. In 1938, his play, *John Brown*, won the Maxwell Anderson Award for Verse Drama; its presentation on a national radio broadcast was a thrilling event in my young life. About twenty-five years later I was living in Vienna and for the first time took opera seriously enough to consider writing one. My thoughts immediately turned to John Brown. It was ten more years, however, before I had the time and nerve to tackle such a formidable subject. I asked my father to make a libretto from his play, which he gladly did although he was over eighty. Meanwhile I began to steep myself in the John Brown literature. The more I read the more I diverged from the concept of my father's play, and after many heartbreaking attempts to reconcile the irreconcilable, we gave it up.

I went on to compose a different opera, writing my own libretto based on Molière's *Tartuffe*. The satisfaction this gave me emboldened me to try *John Brown* again, this time as my own librettist, basing the opera not upon my father's play but upon my own perception of the man and his time. My father's play, while representing many of the various currents of thought around John Brown, viewed him as a loner; it was a poetic psychiatric study buttressed by his discussions with his old Topeka friend, the late, famous psychiatrist Karl Menninger, who pronounced Brown (on scant evidence) paranoiac. My libretto could not have been written without my father's play, but while acknowledging my tremendous debt, I must say that our works are fundamentally different in many respects.

Much research has been done that my father did not have access to. My reading convinced me that Brown was by no means an eccentric ripple in the pool of history, but the crest of a wave so great that we are still in its trough. I also became convinced that in operatic terms, this epochal quality, this "national and religious birthpang," would be an asset. I welcomed a subject which, like *Boris Godunov*, would involve the chorus at every point in the story. I really wanted two choruses, one black and one white, but soon realized that this was virtually impossible. I greatly regretted this loss, because African-Americans are at the very center of the story—not as the problem, as some would have it, but the victims. I decided to give Frederick Douglass a central role and to make individual blacks as prominent as possible.

But this is the story of John Brown, not of Frederick Douglass, which is a great but different story. Nor is this the story of the oppressed slaves, thousands upon thousands of whom risked their lives to escape slavery and later fought for the freedom of their people with great distinction in the Civil War. To show John Brown as a man who "delivered" slaves in no way implies that they did not fight for themselves, witness the many slave rebellions long before John Brown's raid. But Brown was one of the few white men who willingly gave his life to help destroy slavery before the war, and he had the prophetic vision to know exactly what his actions and his death would achieve. For this he has become the greatest white hero to millions of African-Americans, and a hero to people struggling for freedom everywhere.

The opera was originally much longer than it is now. The most difficult scene to cut—and it was not cut until after the premiere—was set in Concord, Massachusetts. I wanted the audience to see Brown supported by Ralph Waldo Emerson and Henry Thoreau. Most of his financial support came from prominent American intellectuals and businessmen in the Boston area. This is unknown to most people today, who cling to the false stereotype of Brown as a lone, bloodthirsty fanatic. Opera, however, cannot tell complete, complex stories. It must concentrate on the essentials in order to make room for music and drama. I can only hope that my picture of John Brown—even without the Concord scene—is sufficiently nuanced to evoke the complicated man he really was.

One aspect of writing the libretto was a particular challenge—how to explain John Brown, but still give vigorous expression to the Southern point of view. Any serious work about John Brown must also be a study of why the Civil War was fought. I did what I could to make it clear that the entire South felt its constitutionally protected rights were being trampled by the North. Even to most people in the North, these rights were infinitely more important than the lives of slaves. Today, when television facilitates instant, visceral compassion for human suffering all over the world, it is hard for us to imagine that before the Civil War so many Americans could simply ignore the barbarous treatment of four million people in their own country. John Brown could not, and though I have tried to dramatize the South's terrible dilemma, Brown can only be understood in his own Calvinist, Old Testament terms—good and evil, freedom and slavery.

Religion—Calvinist and otherwise—was a powerful force in nineteenth-century American life. John Brown was not unique in knowing much of the Bible by heart, but he also believed that it was a guide to action. If Moses killed a slave master to rescue the slave, if Gideon followed God's battle plan, if even Jesus, in the book of Matthew, came "not to send peace, but a sword," then how could he, John Brown, God's miserable servant, look upon this great evil without literally fighting against it? The Bible was real, and so were those millions of suffering human beings in this land that Brown passionately loved. He could not look away; he saw them, he knew them as friends, brothers, sisters. This is what set him apart from most Americans—his utter lack of color phobia in what was a thoroughly racist society.

But religion and race are not so hard for us to understand as many other conditions of that time. As Richard Boyer has written:

> With the time and its temper stripped away—its duels and shootings and assaults, its go-to-hell bravado, its frequent persistence in bringing almost any dispute to mortal encounter, its readiness for martyrdom and pistols at twenty paces, its long cold war over slavery, its private armies and filibustering—with all this gone, John Brown's acts may seem strange to the point of psychosis. With this framing them, however, they are distressingly representative of a tragic and violent age. If the time and its temperament were seldom indicated in accounts of John Brown, neither was the quality of slavery, nor the black man's valiant and repeated attempts for freedom, nor the long and excruciating tension within the lives of many Americans, from Washington to Lincoln, committed to the founding premise that all men were created equal while enslaving millions of their fellow countrymen. Thus the basic social dynamic thrusting John Brown,

his associates, and opponents into history has seldom been emphasized in the story of that long-maturing crisis that he and his famous colleagues, black and white, brought to explosion. Prominent and successful men do not enter such a plot as John Brown's without a social and national history impelling them to it.

In the twentieth century, the tragedy of Nazi Germany was similar. A core of barbarity, however small at first, had the power to corrupt an entire land and leave a legacy of guilt upon all, even the innocent. If there is any "message" here, it must be that if evil is allowed to take root, its consequences will be both terrible and uncontrollable. Or in the words of W. E. B. Du Bois, "The cost of liberty is less than the price of repression." As the world grows smaller and the instruments of destruction more terrible, so does the penalty for repression grow more terrible. We have no guarantee of infinite time here on earth. We must finally learn that injustice is the mother of catastrophe. Our Civil War should teach us that even "unthinkable" wars do indeed happen.

In this discussion I do not wish to give the impression that I claim to have done original research on John Brown or to have put forth original ideas about him. It is hard enough to write an opera without that. Fortunately, there are now a number of excellent books which not only give well documented history, but which examine controversial issues from the viewpoints of different "major premises."

When I wrote my opera, the best biography of John Brown was *To Purge This Land with Blood* by Stephen B. Oates, who has also written a small volume of essays, *Our Fiery Trial*, which describes the fascinating treatment that John Brown, Nat Turner and Abraham Lincoln have received from historians and writers down through the years. *The Legend of John Brown*, by Richard O. Boyer, contains a wealth of information about the issues and personalities of the period. Two recent well-researched and insightful books about John Brown are: *Fire from The Midst of You* by Louis A. DeCaro, Jr. (2002), and *Patriotic Treason* by Evan Carton (2006), which make use of material that has come to light since the previously mentioned biographies were published. DeCaro's book concentrates on Brown's religious life; Carton's has the sweep of a novel; it humanizes Brown and convincingly shows that he acted on the principles of America's founding fathers.

But as I said, opera goers will probably not take the time to read these books. They may, however, still want to know what became of some of the characters who survived. Frederick Douglass continued to be the outstanding spokesman for his race until his death in 1895, having been an adviser to Lincoln and later Minister to Haiti; he bought Robert E. Lee's home. General J. E. B. Stuart was killed in action in 1864. Martha Brown and her baby died within three months of John Brown's hanging. Owen Brown escaped from Harpers Ferry; he later became a grape grower, then moved to California. Annie Brown went to Virginia after the Civil War and taught school to black children in a mansion that had belonged to Governor Wise. In 1866, when the irony of his being refused admission to the house was pointed out to him, the man who ordered Brown's execution is reported to have meditated a moment and then replied, "John Brown was a great man, Sir. John Brown was a hero."

And yet it has not been my intention to portray Brown as a simple "hero." I see this not as an heroic story but as a warning: wherever cruel injustice becomes law, a John Brown will rise up to attack that law by any means. If I show him sometimes as a messianic prophet, it is because that is how Brown finally saw himself, and how his intensely loyal family, companions and supporters saw him. His resolute Calvinist faith was a crucial part of his personality and of the Puritan society he grew up in.

Finally, however, I must recognize the truth of what Stephen Oates writes in the preface to his biography: "Because he is controversial, anybody who ventures forth with a study of his life—no matter how fair-minded and well-researched it may be—is going to encounter a number of readers, critics, and professional historians who have already made up their minds that Brown was either (1) a vicious fanatic, a horse thief, and a maniac or (2) the greatest abolitionist hero in history, and [they] will furiously attack any book that does not argue their point of view."

Oates has "sought to show why Brown performed his controversial deeds rather than to damn or praise him." I follow his example and hope that the addition of music will bring this drama to life in a new and cathartic way. For all my concern with history and drama, I am neither historian nor poet and have from the beginning been acutely aware that an opera lives or dies by the quality of its music. Here I gladly give up words and turn over the consideration of that enigmatic and timeless old man to the hearts and minds of my listeners.

APPENDIX C

Confessions of a Hymn Bandit: The Amazing Case of "Blow Ye the Trumpet"

From the Chorus America magazine Voice, *Spring 2004*

According to legend, Rossini claimed he could set a laundry list to music. I have done something even more embarrassing. I recently discovered that I had inadvertently written a choral piece to a text that is nothing but a list of hymn titles. Don't laugh; it has sold over 50,000 copies and is probably in the repertory of most Chorus America members.

The piece is "Blow Ye the Trumpet" (for mixed, men's or women's chorus) from my opera *John Brown*; it is also used in my suite from the opera, *Songs of the Slave*. I found the text in the fine biography of Brown by Stephen B. Oates, *To Purge This Land with Blood*. I wrote this note for the published music:

> "Blow Ye the Trumpet" was the name of Brown's favorite hymn. A number of different hymn tunes and verses have this same title. As I have been unable to discover which version Brown knew, I have chosen the text I found most beautiful and appropriate—indeed, prophetic—for his life and death. It seems to prophesy both the day of jubilee and the martyr's death which Brown knew would hasten the destruction of slavery. None of the existing hymn tunes fit these

words, however, so I gave them a new melody in the style of early
American folk music."

Here is the text as it appears at the end of Oates's biography:

> Blow ye the trumpet, blow.
> Sweet is Thy work, my God, my King.
> I'll praise my Maker with all my breath.
> O happy is the man who hears.
> Why should we start, and fear to die;
> With songs and honors sounding loud!
> Ah, lovely appearance of death.

Maybe I should have suspected that this was not an authentic hymn
text. It doesn't scan or rhyme, and all the research I did in old hymnals
turned up nothing like it. But I knew that in past centuries, hymns, like
folk songs, acquired many different versions through oral dissemina-
tion. And these words sounded to me like authentic hymn sentiments
that John Brown would have loved, and indeed they were. In a sense,
the old abolitionist wrote his own hymn posthumously, with a little help
from his daughter Ruth, from Franklin Sanborn, Stephen Oates, and
yours truly. Here's what happened.

When Oates was doing research for his book, he consulted the early
biography (1885) by Franklin Sanborn. Sanborn had known John
Brown and his family well, and had asked the surviving children to write
recollections of their father for his book. Ruth Brown Thompson sent
Sanborn a list of the first lines of Brown's favorite hymns, beginning
with "Blow ye the trumpet, blow." They appear on page 39 of Sanborn's
biography. Oates now admits that somehow this list got compressed; it
looked like the lines of a single hymn and that's the way he printed it.

In reality those seven lines are the beginnings of six different hymns,
many by Isaac Watts (1674–1748) and by Charles Wesley (1707–1788),
who wrote the words to the best known hymn with this title. Two of
them (including "Blow Ye") are in the Sacred Harp collection. The texts
and tunes I found for "Blow Ye" are austere and square, quite different
from the free and ecstatic serendipitous text I used, and in no way do
they match its personal and prophetic nature. For all these reasons I
was greatly disappointed when I could not find a single setting of the
mythical text I wanted to use. That is why I decided to write my own

setting of the text found in Oates. It seemed so important to me as a symbol of John Brown's beliefs and personality, that it was the first music I composed for the opera. I had already built the hymn text into the libretto so that it would recur at a number of crucial points, and the melody came to me while I was taking a walk.

Do I now regret Oates's mistake and my perpetuation of it? Not in the least. I regard it as proof that serendipity—or a mistake if you want to call it that—can be heaven sent. That text inspired me. I have composed very few pieces that have occasioned so much emotional response from listeners. After all, these lines *did* represent John Brown's deepest sentiments. It is amazing that the separate titles go together so well, but it should not surprise us that the end result is a concentrated and even poetic picture of a righteous man happy to die in the belief that his death would help end the terrible tragedy of slavery. And it did.

* * *

I am indebted to Greg Artzner for uncovering many of these facts. Greg and Terry Leonino are singing actors who tour under the name of Magpie.

ACKNOWLEDGMENTS

Among the friends and colleagues who have offered sound advice while I wrote this book are Arthur Bloomfield, Deborah Charness, Dr. Michael Charness, Marilyn Chase, Dr. Randolph Chase, Cynthia and Philippe Dunoyer, Dianne Nicolini, Eliza Rubenstein, Suzanne Ryan, Carl Schmidt, and Dorothy Bradford Wexler. My daughter, Elizabeth Carroll, a professional writer and teacher, has given me invaluable help. My other children, Katie, Edward, and Jennifer, have also been supportive and helpful. Bennett Graff, senior editor at Rowman & Littlefield, has by his patience and professional acumen been indispensable. My wife, Donata Coletti Mechem, has suffered through every up and down of this book's checkered history; without her unwavering love and belief in me, neither the book nor many of the events it describes would have happened.

INDEX

ABOUT THE AUTHOR

Kirke Lewis Mechem was born in Wichita, Kansas, and raised in Topeka, the third of four children of an author, Kirke Field Mechem, and a
concert pianist, Katharine Lewis Mechem. He attended public schools,
served in the U.S. Army from 1943 to 1946, and received a BA from
Stanford and an MA from Harvard. He taught and conducted at Menlo
College, Stanford University, and the University of San Francisco before becoming a freelance composer in 1970. He married Donata Coletti in 1955; they still live in the same house in San Francisco where
they brought up four children.